# Zen and The Art of Foosball

A Zen Games Book

# Zen and The Art of Foosball

## A Beginner's Guide to Table Soccer

Charles C. Lee
with David Richard and Attma Sharma

Writers Club Press
San Jose  New York  Lincoln  Shanghai

Zen and The Art of Foosball
A Beginner's Guide to Table Soccer

Writers Club Press
an imprint of iUniverse, Inc.

For information address:
iUniverse, Inc.
5220 S. 16th St., Suite 200
Lincoln, NE 68512
www.iuniverse.com

This book does not guarantee enlightenment.

ISBN: 0-595-21705-2

Printed in the United States of America

*This book is dedicated to Mom, Dad, Grace, friends, foosers,
teachers, Lloydies, and various other organisms
in the Milky Way.*

Knowing others is wisdom, knowing yourself is enlightenment
—Lao Tzu


To secure ourselves against defeat lies within our own hands, but the opportunity of defeating the enemy lies within the enemy himself.

—Sun Tzu


Some days you eat the bear, some days the bear eats you.
—Mr. T

# CONTENTS

# LIST OF ILLUSTRATIONS

# PREFACE

*Zen and the Art of Foosball* represents the culmination of several years of playing and learning about the sport of foosball. This sport has provided us with many hours of pleasure and excitement. The moments spent at the tables with good friends and worthy adversaries remain a constant source of entertainment. Now comes the time for us to give something back to the sport.

In fact, there may be those better qualified to offer a beginner's account to the game of foosball. However, there has not been a single new book on the subject since Johnny Lott's seminal work, which is now out of print and out-dated. We offer this as our contribution for others to hopefully expand upon.

This project started several years ago when the Tornado Soccer Table was beginning to make its appearance. For quite some time, professional foosball had been waning. We like most others were excited to see the resurrection of a sport that we personally cherished. Unlike Europe where foosball has a strong and proud tradition, American foosball is just beginning to see its history flourish. Now is a golden era for American foosball, with tournaments and competition reaching record levels. We hope the new initiates to this sport will discover all of the rich pleasures and challenges that lie ahead for foosball.

Happy foosing!

Charles Lee
David Richard
Attma Sharma

*We thank Tornado Soccer and the USTSA.*

*Contributing suggestions were kindly provided by John Haba, Jack Prater, Anatole Faykin, and Jordan Hague.*

# INTRODUCTION

Welcome to the exciting world of foosball! This book is intended as a guide for the beginning player interested in learning how to play foosball. In the following chapters, you will learn the basics of the game, how to pass the ball, shoot the ball, and defend against shots. You will also learn advanced techniques for improving your game. Advanced players will also find useful information for increasing their level of play.

Before long, you may find yourself playing in a professional tournament! In fact, when this book was first written, the United States Table Soccer Association monitored approximately ten thousand individuals in its national ranking system. This number represents a four-fold increase of the player base within a five-year period. In addition, the USTSA conservatively estimates that as many as half a million people play the sport outside the professional circuit, and the number of recreational players may be several million.

So, get ready to join the legion of players discovering a sport that is now in its golden age. This is a sport that the young and old alike can enjoy. And, this is a sport that we hope you will continue to enjoy for years to come.

# Part I

---

# The Ancient Art of Foosball

# CHAPTER 1

## History of the Game

In the late 1800's, **table soccer** or **foosball** (the German word for soccer) was developed in Europe as a response to the widespread love for the field sport of soccer. The development of the game has roots in traditional puppetry, woodwork, and fine craftsmanship. Indeed, the renowned passions of the Old World Europeans for sport and art blended and found unique expression through the invention of foosball. The game enjoyed popularity amongst a wide range of people of all ages and remains an established pastime to this day.

Around the turn of the century, it is believed that European immigrants brought the game to America. However, the game remained widely unknown and unplayed for over half a century. But in 1970, Lee Peppard designed a brand of table that quickly became the standard table of play for over a decade. Its popularity spread internationally and was fueled by the **World Table Soccer Association's** Million-Dollar Tour. It was during this time that foosball gained its highest level of popularity. Tournaments brought contestants from all over the world as top purses reached values as high as a quarter of a million dollars. But almost as quickly as foosball begin to flourish, technological forces were casting an ominous shadow over the future of foosball.

During most of the 1980's, the advent of arcade video games began to replace foosball as a major source of indoor gaming recreation. The WTSA dissolved and the Million Dollar tables were no longer produced. However, the game continued to maintain a loyal legion of enthusiasts and cheaper model tables continued to be sold. It was not until 1988 that professional foosball was revived when **the United States Table Soccer Association** was formed, utilizing the Tornado Soccer table as the official table of play. Since then, the tour has expanded to become the **North American Table Soccer Association** and has grown to over 20,000 members together with sales of foosball tables. The rapid appearance of game tables in arcades, bars, college recreation rooms, and community centers demonstrates the renewed interest in a sport with a remarkable history.

# CHAPTER 2

## Game Tables

Initially, you may be amazed at the array of different tables on which foosball is played, but if you consider the evolution of the game and the craftsmanship employed in the design of the tables, you can begin to appreciate the diversity and special characteristics of each table. It is believed that the first game tables were designed and built in Germany around the late 1800s. These tables were generally poorly constructed by the modern player's standard. However, the basic layout of the table has remained largely unchanged since then.

Foosball tables were thought to have been introduced in the United States as early as the turn of century, perhaps by emigrating Europeans. Manufacturing of foosball tables continued throughout the century, but the models were of widely varying styles and were generally poorly constructed. This was the state of the sport until **Lee Peppard** designed his **Tournament Soccer** line of tables. His goal was to build durable tables made from materials of the highest quality. Because of this, the popularity of the sport grew, more players began to use this table and more interesting styles of play were developed. As a result, it quickly became the standard table of play during the 1970s and early 1980s.

The Tournament Soccer table was constructed of high quality woods and smooth durable plastics. This permitted a controlled yet fast-paced style of play without fear of the table giving way or breaking. However, as more aggressive styles began to develop, it was common for playing figures to break when suitably stressed. The tables came in different sizes, different colored playing surfaces, and tailored for different markets. Among these tables, the one that became most prominent was the brown-topped million-dollar table. A prominent feature of this table was the sloped corners near the goal. And, it is this table which was the official table of the WTSA Million Dollar Tour. As a result, the design of this table has since been widely copied by several other manufacturers.

The efforts of the **Tournament Soccer Company** to provide high-quality, low-cost tables succeeded for a time. However, the demise of the company was brought about by the appearance of electronic video games, which quickly began to replace foosball tables in many locations. Still, the game refused to die, and in the late 1980s, the **Tornado Soccer Company** began producing high quality tables of their own. This created a renaissance in the sport, and a new professional tour was formed that used this table. The table itself is made from higher quality woods and high tech synthetics used for the surfaces and figures. In addition, the overall appearance reflects the sleek, modern style of the game. (Figure 2.1) Unlike the Tournament Soccer tables, the Tornado tables employ three figures on the goalie rod as opposed to sloped corners. In addition, because of the high tolerance, precision-machined parts, the modern game is very fast-paced and requires greater skill to control the ball.

Apart from these two tables, you may also encounter tables manufactured by Dynamo, Bonzini, and Garlando, to name a few. The quality of these tables is generally good and styles developed on one of the major tables can generally be used on them. However, since tables vary in terms of their speed of play and other unique characteristics, some adaptation time should be expected. Since the major table in use today is the Tornado

**Figure 2.1**  A Tornado Table Soccer Table. This is one of the most used types of tables in professional table soccer.

Soccer Table, techniques presented here will be demonstrated with this table in mind, but can be adapted to other tables as well.

# Part II

# Let's Play Ball: The Fundamentals of Playing Foosball

# CHAPTER 3

## First Things First

A good journey always starts with a good beginning. Thus, your enjoyment of foosball will undoubtedly increase once you learn the fundamental rules and techniques of the game. Therefore, the first rule you must learn is that spinning the rods is not allowed. Spinning warps the rods, can damage the rest of the table, and on the whole is less effective then a careful, well-executed shot. The game also becomes more meaningful once you start playing strategically to set-up and execute shots.

Once you heed rule number one, the foosball table becomes more than a series of randomly placed rods with men attached. The layout of the table is in fact well organized. (Figure 3.1) On opposite sides of the cabinet, the goals are guarded by two sets of rods, the **goalie rod** which is closest to the goal and the **two-man rod** which is immediately adjacent. Moving towards the center, the next rod is the opposing team's **three-man rod,** which is also called the **forward rod.** And finally, the next rod is your **five-man rod.** Whether playing in teams or one-on-one, the **defense position** is always manned using the goalie rod and the two-man rod, and the **offense position** is played using the five-man and three-man rods. When playing a **singles game,** a player will often switch between these two positions; however, it is often acceptable to operate positions in between. It is beneficial to stay in these intermediate positions for a short period of time. The techniques used to defend or attack depend upon being in the correct position on the table.

A typical game proceeds in the following manner. A coin is flipped and the winning team chooses either the side of the table or to have the first serve. The players then take their positions and the ball is served into the playing field. If the ball is stopped by one of the team's five-men, the ball must then touch at least two of the five-men without stopping before being passed forward. If the ball does not stop but remains in motion, it can be advanced forward without adhering to the previous rule. A player has 15 seconds to advance the ball from the five-man rod or the other team is allowed to take position and re-serve the ball. Although it is not illegal, attempting to score with the five-man on the first drop is considered rude. If the ball is successfully passed to the player's three-man, the player has ten seconds to shoot the ball into the goal. Often as a beginner, your shot will be blocked or miss the goal completely.

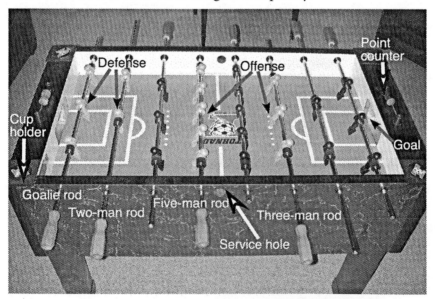

**Figure 3.1** - The layout of a typical foosball table. The ball is served through the service hole. The offense is played using the Five-man and Three-man rods. And, the defense is played by using the Goalie and Two-man rods. The object of the game is to get the ball into the goal.

Assume the shot misses and the defense now has possession of the ball. The defense has 10 seconds to advance the ball forward to the opposite goal. Unlike the previous case with the five-men, if the ball comes to rest and the defense intends to pass it to the three-man or five-man rather than shoot on goal, the defense is not required to have two defending figures touch the ball before passing. If during the game, the ball comes to rest in a location where no one can reach it, then the team that served last is allowed to re-serve the ball. If a team scores, the opposing team is allowed to serve the ball next. If the ball happens to enter the goal but bounces back out, then the point is still counted and the ball served by the other team. However if the ball hits a post and bounces out, the goal is not counted and play resumes. The game continues until five points is reached by either team. This summarizes the most often encountered situations in a simple game of foosball. For more specific rules, an appendix is included which will help you deal with unusual circumstances that may arise during the play of a game.

There are also several unwritten rules of foosball etiquette that you should learn. First, as we mentioned above, never spin the rods on purpose. Many players become absolutely livid when they see this. Second, trash talking is not only against the rules, but it's rude as well. Remember it's only a game. Third, if you are interested in challenging the winner of a game, you should offer to pay for at least half the game. If you lose and want a rematch, you should offer to pay for the whole game. If you happen to be playing a singles game and a team wishes to challenge you and your opponent, you should pair up and both teams should pay for half a game. And of course, last but not least, remember to shake hands after a match.

Now that you have become acquainted with the rules of the game, you will be interested in learning how to actually play. The following chapters describe the basics of the game; i.e. stance, grip, serves, and ball control. And the subsequent sections describe the specifics of defense, passing, and offense. Once these techniques have been mastered, ideas are presented for advancing your level of play. With this information, you will be on the road to mastering the game of foosball.

# CHAPTER 4

## Taking a Stand

As in any sport, one of the fundamental techniques in foosball is the stance. If overlooked when first learning the game, serious problems in shooting, passing, and defending can result. However, developing a proper stance is actually quite simple.

The two basic stances are the open and the closed stance. Among the two, the open stance is the most widely used and the most versatile. This stance is particularly useful in offensive shooting where it promotes the generation of power in the shot by increasing hip and arm motion. The open stance begins by placing your left foot about six inches from the base of the table and pointing your left toe at a 45-degree angle. Situate your body perpendicular to the direction the foot is pointing, and place your right foot a comfortable distance away from the left foot along the bodyline. (Figure 4.1a) Often times, players will use a modified open stance where the right foot is kicked back onto the toe and the body weight gravitates over the left foot. As a result, the torso shifts closer to the table. This aids in seeing the playing surface and also leads to a greater sense of stability. (Figure 4.1b)

In comparison, the **closed stance** begins by placing both of your feet approximately six inches from the table with the toes pointing perpendicular to the table. Align your body parallel to the playing surface. (Figure 4.1c) This closed stance is particularly useful in passing because the equal distribution of body weigh results in greater control of the pass. In certain cases, an **extremely closed stance** is used which is basically a mirror reflection of the modified open stance. (Figure 4.1d) However, its use is limited to a few rare offensive shots, and is discussed in the chapters concerning those shots.

Positioning your body with respect to the rods depends on which position (offense or defense) you are playing and which stance you are using. In general, when using the open stance, your body centers on the rod that the left hand is holding. And, when utilizing the closed stance, the center of your body is located between the rods that your right and left hands are holding.

Of course, as with all techniques, the exact position of the body will vary with the individual. For example, tall players may need to stand further from the table in order to accommodate their longer reach. In all cases, you should experiment with distances and positions so that you can find a comfortable place to take a stand.

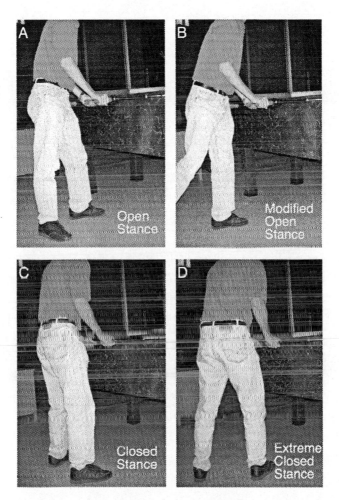

**Figure 4.1** - Four stances used in foosball. **A.** Open Stance. **B.** Modified Open Stance. **C.** Closed Stance. **D.** Extreme Closed Stance.

# CHAPTER 5

## Get a Grip

How you choose to grip the rods affects many aspects of your ability to play foosball. A grip that is too strong may prevent you from generating sufficient power to shoot the ball. And a grip that is too weak often results in poor ball handling and control. The secret is to grip the rods comfortably, yet with authority. This is not to say that the pressure on the rods will always remain constant. For instance, when catching a pass, the pressure on the rods often increases from a loose grip to a tight grip. Conversely, when shooting or passing the ball, the pressure on the rods will often decrease from a tight grip to a loose grip.

There are probably as many different grips as there are players. However, most fall into a variation of one of the following three categories, **the power grip, the golf grip**, and **the palm grip**. In addition, there is a special grip that is used when executing an offensive maneuver called the snake shot that is discussed in Chapter 14. When playing the game, most players will often alternate between grips, since each has its own unique advantages.

**The power grip** is often used in situations where blocking the ball is a priority, such as on defense or blocking a pass with the five-men. Despite its namesake, the power grip actually confers very little power to a shot. It does, however, give moderate rotational flexibility along with a great deal of longitudinal freedom in the rods. This makes it ideal for passing. The grip itself is quite simple. First, place your palm on the handle at about a 45-degree angle. Then, wrap your fingers and thumb around the handle as if you were making a fist. (Figure 5.1 a) To advance the ball from this position involves utilizing a screwdriver-like motion with a whip-like finish to generate power. In order to get a feel for this motion, pretend as if you are screwing in a screw that is stuck but suddenly gives way. This motion is called a **wrist flick**. (Figure 5.1b-c)

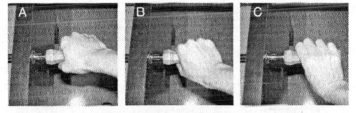

**Figure 5.1 - A.** The Power Grip. This grip provides low rotational flexibility and excellent stability for handling the rods. **B-C.** Wrist flick with the power grip. This movement generates very little power and is best for passing the ball.

**Figure 5.2 - A.** The Golf Grip. This grip provides moderate rotational flexibility and moderate stability for handling the rods. **B-C.** Wrist flick with the golf grip. This movement generates a large amount of power and is good for passing and shooting the ball.

**Figure 5.3 - A.** The Palm Grip. This grip provides excellent rotational flexibility and low stability for handling the rods. **B-C.** Palm roll with the palm grip. This movement generates the most power of the three grips, however it is awkward for manipulating the ball. It is best used for shooting the ball.

The golf grip is very similar to the power grip, but the added rotational flexibility of the golf grip is useful when making shots from the three-man rod. The grip itself is very similar to an actual golf grip where the middle, ring, and pinkie fingers have the most contact with the handle. The handle is cradled in these three fingers while the thumb and index finger remain loosely pinched together. (Figure 5.2a) Advancing the ball with the right hand involves using the wrist flick with an additional movement where your thumb and pinkie release their grip. Thrust your wrist downward and the handle will roll into your cupped fingers. (Figure 5.2b-c) The same is true for movement with the left hand, however your hand moves upward as your wrist moves laterally towards the body. These motions can be reversed for the hands to advance the ball backwards.

The palm grip is one of the least used grips due to the inability of most players to have much finesse control with it. Despite this disadvantage, using this method with a palm roll gives a great deal of power to a shot. It is also a grip that is distinctly different for the right and left hands. For the right hand, place the handle in the center of your palm with your hands open and your fingers curled upwards. (Figure 5.3 a) Striking the ball involves a downward wind-up followed by an upward strike while catching the handle in your fingertips. (Figure 5.3 b-c) For the left hand, the handle is placed in the middle of your fingers on a completely open hand. There is an opposite upward wind-up followed by a downward strike where your fingers roll-up behind the grip in order to catch it. If done properly, this can create a great deal of power.

Initially, practicing these various grips may feel quite awkward. In addition, most beginners find that it can be very difficult to generate power without inadvertently releasing the rods. But, as your wrists loosen up and develop more snap, a powerful shot will easily be within your grasp. Just remember to relax and get a grip.

# CHAPTER 6

## Service with a Smile

In an official game, after the initial coin toss, the team that won the toss may either choose to serve the ball or to have a specific side of the table. The game then begins with the ball served by the winning team. This team may use any legal technique to serve the ball to their own five-men, and thus take immediate possession of the served ball. Alternatively, in an unofficial game, the game may begin without a coin toss and with a fair serve of the ball by the team that is on the side of the ball return. A **fair serve** is one that does not give an initial advantage to either side, and there should be no attempt to serve the ball to one's own side. This type of serve may involve simply throwing the ball randomly through the service hole. However, after a point is scored, the side that lost the point is allowed to influence the next serve in order to take possession of the ball. Hands are not allowed in the playing field *during* or *after* the serve, but may be in the field to position the ball *before* the serve.

For tables with a **service cup**, the following technique may be used to serve the ball to your own side. Place the ball on the top left edge of the cup and then release it slowly. The ball will spiral down the side of the cup and enter the table rolling toward your five-men. The exact trajectory that the ball takes will depend on the initial position of the ball on the lip of the cup. With practice, you can accurately predict where the ball will land with each serve.

For tables lacking the service cup, a different technique is required. First, place the ball into the service hole. Then serve the ball by placing your thumb on the left side of the ball and imparting backspin with a downward stroke while pushing the ball to the right. (Figure 6.1) The ball will bounce off the right edge of the hole and cross over the center to land on your side of the table. The backspin will cause the ball to stop and roll back as soon as it hits the surface of the table. Unlike the previous serve, practice is required to perfect this technique, but an assiduous student can master it within a few hours and will quickly find themselves serving their opponent with a smile.

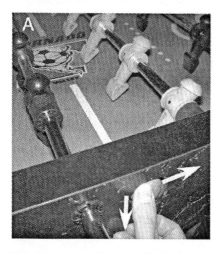 

**Figure 6.1 - A.** Serving the ball with backspin. By simultaneously applying forward pressure and downward spin, the ball will enter the playing field and then spin back toward your figures. **B.** The ball will typically approach your first or second five-man.

# CHAPTER 7

## Pinning the Ball

Once the ball is in play, you will find that randomly flailing the playing figures at the ball is unpredictable and inefficient. In order to increase your probability of successfully hitting the ball into the goal, you will need to develop a repertoire of passing and shooting techniques. However, you can not do this until you are able to stop and control the ball. This chapter deals with methods for stopping the ball and setting it up for a shot. The following chapter deals with methods for effectively learning how to control the ball.

In order to stop a ball that is coming at one of your playing figures, you should angle the figure slightly away from the direction in which the ball is coming. When the ball strikes the surface of the figure, release a slight amount of pressure on the handle so that the momentum can be absorbed by the playing figure. If done properly, the ball will come to rest trapped beneath the playing figure in either a **front-pin** or **back-pin** depending upon the direction which the ball was coming. (Figure 7.1c,d)

At this point, the ball may not be securely positioned and could easily slip away from the figure. A tight pin position is one where the point of contact of the playing figure's toe is directly on top of the ball. This gives a total downward force and leaves no lateral force that could cause the ball to slip. To obtain this position, you will have to tweak the position of the ball using very subtle motions. One method is to alternate between the front-pin and back-pin by imparting a slight forward momentum to the ball. To do this, push the toe of the playing figure around the top of the ball (either clockwise or counterclockwise) with enough pressure so that the ball moves forward slowly. (Figure 7.1) Wait until the ball moves under the playing figure on the opposite side and pin the ball again. If the ball is almost secure, tap the ball slightly to jostle it into position.

After stopping the ball, you may want to move it to a better location. This is easily accomplished by sliding the toe of the playing figure across the top of the ball. (Figure 7.1) The ball will roll longitudinally beneath the rod. When it reaches the correct location, stop it by pinning the ball and re-securing it as above.

This is perhaps one of the most difficult aspects for a beginner to learn, and as such it requires a great deal of patience and practice. It is easy to become quite frustrated by a ball slipping out of position. But don't be discouraged. And remember that pinning the ball effectively is essential to *all* elements of foosball.

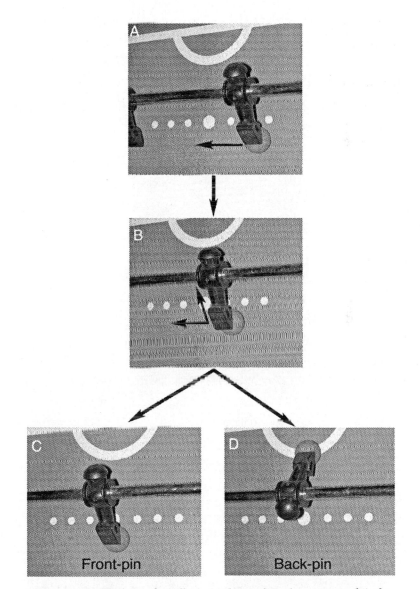

**Figure 7.1** - Manipulating the ball. **A.** Applying a lateral movement while the ball is pinned will start the ball rolling. **B.** Continuing laterally or applying a rotational torque to the ball will respectively result in a front-pin (**C**) or back-pin (**D**).

# CHAPTER 8

## Take Control

In fact, there may be no adequate way of describing ball control. It is as much feel as it is technique, if not more so. However, there are some drills and elements that all players can use to improve their feel for manipulating the ball.

The major focus when learning how to control the ball is to pay attention to the physical movements of the ball on the table. How does the ball roll in certain situations? How does the surface of the table affect pinning the ball? Is it slippery or rough? How does the ball rebound off the walls? How does the ball behave when the playing figure contacts it in a certain way? These may seem like basic questions, but paying attention to these elements will improve your ability to predict how the ball will behave.

To further develop this intuitive feel for the table, you should spend time alone manipulating the ball. A good drill is to practice pin positions as described in the previous chapter. Another useful method is to throw the ball into the playing area at random and try to bring the ball to rest in a particular location. This could involve first stopping the ball, then passing the ball between various playing figures. A useful drill is to pass the ball back and forth between figures on the same rod and then on different rods. Another useful drill is to repeatedly hit the ball with the three man rod against the goalie wall. These drills can be very useful for developing your reflex and finesse control. Also, if you have the opportunity, you should watch other players handle the ball. Often times, watching advanced players will give you ideas on how to improve your own ability to handle the ball.

One final note on ball control. It may be possible to become very adept at playing on one type of table, but have less agility on a different table, as in tennis where there are clay and grass court specialists. Some players may be able to adapt to new surfaces very quickly. One way of adapting to a different table is to treat the tables as essentially the same but only make minor modifications. The common differences among tables are the shape of the figures, the type of ball, and the texture of the playing surface. Generally, the shape of the figures will only affect the pin position, and the type of ball and playing surface will affect the speed of the table. The first is definitely the hardest part to adjust. But, making a slight modification to the rotation of the playing figure will often do the trick.

With practice you will quickly adapt to all types of tables and show everyone how to take control.

# Part III

# From Here to There: The Passing Game

# CHAPTER 9

## The Importance of Passing

The ultimate focus in foosball is to put the ball into the opposing team's goal. This can best be accomplished with a shot placed precisely around the other team's defending figures. Naturally, this is most easily done by shooting with the three-man rod, since there are fewer opposing figures to bypass. So, every time you get the ball to your three-man rod, you have a better opportunity to score. However, getting the ball to the three-man rod can be quite difficult if you do not have a specific method for passing the ball. As you may have noticed, the three-man rod is unique in that it is the only rod that is located on the opponent's side of the court. Thus, you are at a disadvantage since you only have control of 25% of the playing field on that side. (Figure 9.1) Consequently, it is far more likely that a ball struck randomly into your opponent's side of the court will wind up under the control of one of your opponent's men. In addition, your three-man rod is situated between two of the opposing player's rods, i.e. the opponent's five-man and two-man rods. So, there is a premium placed on directing the ball precisely to your three-man rod.

Because of this premium placed on a precise pass, you will find several chapters here which detail a number of different techniques for passing the ball. Most of these involve passes from the five-man rod to the three-man rod. These are the highest percentage passes since there is only one opposing rod to bypass. However, a few passes from the two-man rod to the three-man rod are covered as well.

Although the passes described in the following chapters have been shown to work extremely well, you should not focus too much on the pass itself when actually playing. Often, a player will begin to focus too intently on the mechanics of passing. As a result, he will inadvertently pass the ball straight to the opposing player. At all times, you should remember to pay attention to the opponent's figures and look for the gaps in his defense. The techniques described will merely help you exploit your opponent's weaknesses. However, if you happen to observe a gap in the defense before you set up a pass, you should quickly take the opportunity to pass the ball.

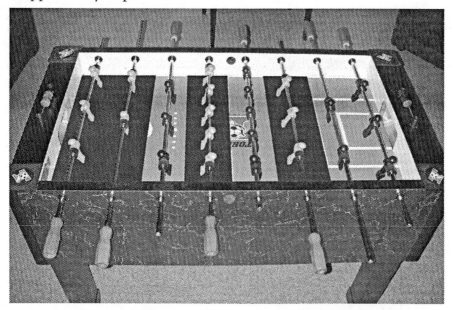

**Figure 9.1** - Areas controlled by playing figures. The areas controlled by the light team have been darkened. Notice that the three-man rod only controls one-quarter of the area on the dark team's side. Consequently, accurate passing is required to deliver the ball to the forward rod.

In short, passing is a dynamic process. It involves continually assessing the opponent's position and adjusting to it. Consequently, you should always be adapting techniques to the particular game you are playing. And finally, don't forget to catch the ball. A perfectly placed pass will be useless if you fail to catch the ball. Try to keep all of this in mind as you learn the following techniques.

# CHAPTER 10

## Just Passing Through

When first learning foosball, it is easy to focus on developing a deadly offense while neglecting to perfect an equally lethal passing game. However, a killer shot will be useless if you can not advance the ball to your three-man rod. Consequently, it is essential that you acquire fundamental passing skills from the start. As a first step in gaining these skills, you should learn the simple yet effective **slide series**, composed of the **wall pass** and the **lane pass**. Like all skilled passes, these will exploit the area between the wall and the second five-man, since this region contains the largest area guarded by a single defending figure.

Without a doubt, the easiest pass to learn in the slide series is the **wall pass**. This pass is initiated by setting the ball on the inside edge of the second five-man and by deploying the inside forward snugly against the wall. (Figure 10.1a) As soon as the ball reaches the wall, pass it forward to the waiting three-man. (Figure 10.1b) To aid in catching passes, especially fast ones, it is imperative that you angle the three-man rod slightly forward. In this position, the inside three-man will absorb most of the ball's momentum and prevent the pass from ricocheting away.

Unfortunately, the wall pass is insufficient by itself since your opponent can easily leave his far five-man camped out on the wall. However, with the addition of the **lane pass**, the ball can be theoretically advanced

100% of the time. As opposed to the wall pass, the lane pass will travel between your opponent's first and second five-men. Once again, set the ball on the inside edge of the second five-man. Now, pull and cock the five-man rod while simultaneously moving the near forward two ball-lengths off the wall. As soon as the ball is aligned with the near forward, drive the ball through. (Figure 10.1c)

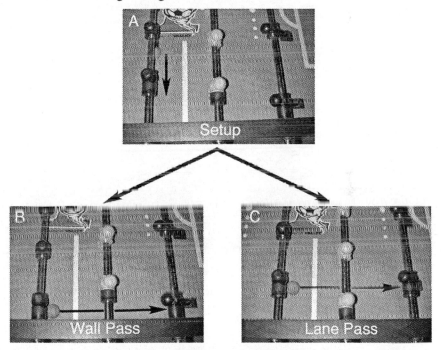

**Figure 10.1** - The Slide Series. **A.** The setup position involves placing the ball on the inside of the second five-man. The ball is then set in motion towards the wall. **B.** The wall pass involves passing the ball once it has reached the wall. **C.** The lane pass involves passing the ball before it has reached the wall.

It is important to note that this pass series is not limited to the near side of the table; it is just as effective on the far side. In this instance, begin by positioning the ball on the outside of the fourth five-man. All the motions are the same except you push the ball toward the near wall.

When executing this pass series, you should concentrate on maintaining the same speed for both the wall pass and the lane pass to guarantee that your opponent will not anticipate which option you will take. Finally, with attention to detail and regular practice, you will be able to tell your opponent that you're "just passing through."

# CHAPTER 11

# One Good Pass Deserves Another

Although it is possible to know just the slide series, the chances of the defender anticipating the wall or lane pass becomes greater with each successive pass. This is because the wall and lane passes are inherently different in the distance the ball must travel before being struck. So, even though it is possible to disguise the initial push from the second five-man, there will always be some small difference between the passes that can be detected in order to block the intended pass. Simply put, limiting yourself to two passes makes it easier for the defender to figure out what you're going to do.

One way to create unpredictability in your passes is by adding several new passes to your arsenal. In this respect, there are three options that you can add to the slide series. These passes are collectively known as **turnaround passes,** and individually are the **wall bounce-pass, the lane-angled pass, and the five-man turnaround.** Alternatively, one can attempt to retool with a completely different arsenal of passes. This arsenal is called the **brush pass series** and if done correctly can completely mask the direction of the pass.

First, we will consider the advanced **turnaround passes** for the slide series. These passes are called turnarounds because they start moving towards one hole and turnaround towards another. The basic turnaround option for the wall-slide pass is the **wall-bounce pass** and is executed in exactly the same fashion as the wall-slide pass. However, instead of passing the ball at the wall, allow the ball to bounce off the wall. Simultaneously, bring the near five-man off the wall and pass the ball through the lane. (Figure 11.1a,c,d)

Similarly, the turnaround pass for the lane pass, **the lane-angled pass**, starts off as a lane pass and turns around into a wall pass. Beginning like a lane slide pass, contact the ball instead on the far corner so that it is shot at an angle towards the wall. The ball will rebound off the wall at an angle so the three-man must be brought off the wall in order to catch it. (Figure 11.1b)

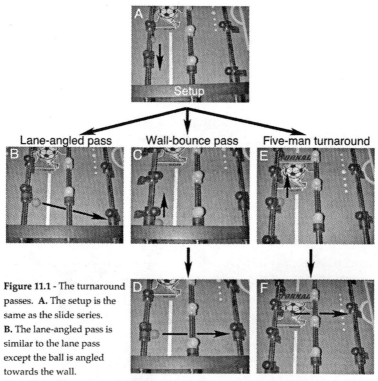

Figure 11.1 - The turnaround passes. **A.** The setup is the same as the slide series. **B.** The lane-angled pass is similar to the lane pass except the ball is angled towards the wall. **C-D.** The wall bounce pass is similar to the wall pass except the ball bounces off of the wall and is hit through the lane. **E-F.** The five-man turnaround is unique in that the ball is first passed to the middle five-man before being passed forward.

Finally, **the five-man turnaround** is a turnaround that does not involve either the wall or lane pass. The initial setup is like the start of the slide series, but instead the second five-man quickly passes it to the middle five-man which in turn passes it to the middle three-man (Figure 11.1e-f). The trick in this turnaround is to create the impression that the initial movement around the ball looks like the beginning of a slide series pass.

All of the above turnaround passes require timing in order to adequately misdirect the defender. For instance, in the wall-bounce pass, moving off the wall too early can signal the intent of the pass. Timing is essential to all of the turnarounds and varies among players. So, experiment with timing the passes differently to see what works best for you.

Now, we shall consider the **brush-pass series**. This pass series takes a different approach from the slide series and turnarounds. Rather than relying on a quick pass from the second five-man, the brush pass uses a slow moving pass to the near five-man who then quickly passes it through either the wall or lane from an intermediate position using a brush stroke.

**The brush pass** begins by loosely back-pinning the ball with the second five-man. The ball should be in a position such that it is on the verge of slipping out of the pin. Slowly set the ball in motion toward the near wall by pulling the rod slowly towards you. (Figure 11.2a) As the ball is in motion, move the near five-man slightly off the ball and follow the ball as it moves. At this point, you must begin **the brush stroke**. This involves rapidly moving the five-man back and forth behind the ball. (Figure 11.2b) The brush stroke covers less than half-an-inch behind the ball and should oscillate very rapidly.

When the ball has reached a position between the wall and lane, it is time to pass the ball. To execute a **wall-brush pass**, bring the oscillating five-man into contact with the ball and make a final pull towards the near wall in order to impart spin on the ball. At the same time, apply a small amount of forward pressure, and the ball will spin along the wall where it can be caught by your three-man (Figure 11.2 c). A lane brush-pass is executed using a brush stroke towards the far wall while applying a slight amount of forward pressure. The ball will spin off to the lane where it can be caught. (Figure 11.2d)

The brush pass requires a great deal of practice, since the brush stroke is difficult to master. However, the advantage is that the brushing motions behind the ball combined with the fact that the ball can be passed to either the wall or lane from the same place makes the pass difficult to predict and results in an especially powerful pass.

With all of these passes added to your arsenal, you may have difficulty deciding which pass to use. As always, you should work on the passes you feel most comfortable with, and resort to the other passes on an interim basis. This is not to say that you shouldn't practice the other passes, since you never know when you might need one. After all, one good pass deserves another.

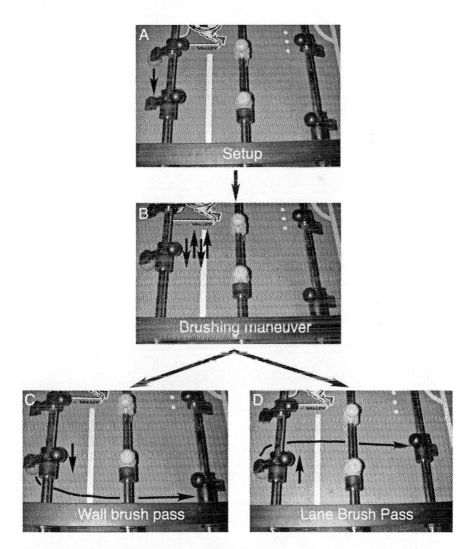

**Figure 11.2** - The Brush Pass Series. **A.** The ball is setup in a back-pin on the second five-man and passed to the first five-man. **B.** The first five-man oscillates rapidly behind the ball. **C.** Applying a brush stroke towards the wall will cause the ball to spin toward the wall. **D.** Applying a brush toward the lane will cause the ball to spin toward the lane.

# CHAPTER 12

## It Takes Two to Tango

So far, we have concerned ourselves with passes from the five-man rod to the three-man rod. However, you can not expect to always have control of the ball on the offensive rods. In fact, it is more likely that as a beginner the ball will be in your possession on the defensive rods. From the defense position, you have two options, either to shoot the ball or to pass it. As mentioned before, the highest percentage shots take place from the three-man rod. Consequently, passing is the preferred alternative in team play. This is not to say that you should never shoot the ball from defense. For instance, in singles play, shooting from the defense may be a more viable option. Nevertheless, an effective pass from the defense to either the five-man or three-man rods can set up a higher percentage scoring opportunity. It is important to note that many of the same rules that apply in five-man to three-man passing also apply here. Most importantly, a stopped ball can not be directly passed from defense to the five-man rod; oddly, this rule does not apply to a pass to the three-man rod.

The **Tango Pass Series** is a useful series of passes from defense has the options of passing to either the five-man rod or the three-man rod. Simply, the pass series is set up as follows. Position the three-man rod snugly against the far wall, and place the far five-man, far two-man, and far goalie-man two ball-lengths from the far wall with the ball loosely front-pinned by the far two-man. (Figure 12.1a) It is important to line up the ball such that only the opponent's near three-man is able to cover the passing area. Of course, this series of passes can also be done using the near wall. The advantage of using the far wall is that your opponent's line of sight is obscured.

From the set up position, the ball must be passed to another defender before it can be passed forward. This is accomplished by passing the ball back to the goalie rod. From here, it's possible to pass the ball forward to the waiting five-man. (Figure 12.1b) However, if the three-man is guarding the lane, then the ball should be passed back and forth between the two-man and the goalie rods in a process known as **dribbling**. If the lane opens up, then the ball can be passed from the goalie-rod as before. Alternatively, it can be passed from the two-man by first slowing the ball down, then sliding around to the back of the ball and passing it forward. (Figure 12.1c)

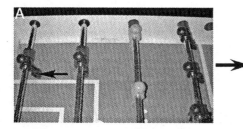

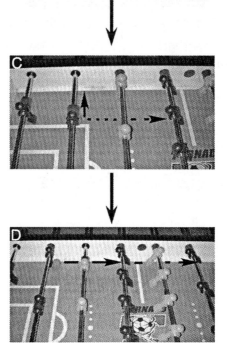

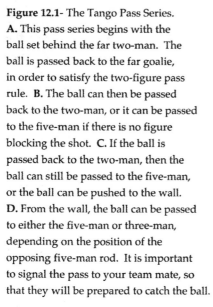

**Figure 12.1-** The Tango Pass Series.
**A.** This pass series begins with the ball set behind the far two-man. The ball is passed back to the far goalie, in order to satisfy the two-figure pass rule. **B.** The ball can then be passed back to the two-man, or it can be passed to the five-man if there is no figure blocking the shot. **C.** If the ball is passed back to the two-man, then the ball can still be passed to the five-man, or the ball can be pushed to the wall. **D.** From the wall, the ball can be passed to either the five-man or three-man, depending on the position of the opposing five-man rod. It is important to signal the pass to your team mate, so that they will be prepared to catch the ball.

Naturally, the lane will not open up unless there is a second option to the pass, and this second option is a **push pass** to the wall. In effect, when the ball is dribbled to the two-man, slow the ball down with the two-man. Then, slide the two-man around the ball to the near side and push the ball to the far wall to trap the ball. Slide the two-man around the back of the ball and pass it to the five-man that is simultaneously moved against the wall to catch the pass. (Figure 12.1c-d) It is important to make both the lane and wall pass from the two-man seem indistinguishable when the ball is being passed by the two-man.

The three-man rod comes into play during the wall pass, if you notice that the defender's five-man is not guarding the wall. In this case, rather than catching with the five-man, lift the five-man and let the ball travel all the way to the three-man. (Figure 12.1d) Similarly, a lane pass to the three-man can be done if the defender's five-man is not in the lane. However, this pass requires some skill to catch because the speed and distance the ball is traveling makes positioning the three-man extremely difficult.

Since you will usually be attempting to utilize this pass series in doubles competition, it is important that you signal your teammate with information about which pass to expect. Obviously, any hand or vocal signals can be intercepted and decoded, so an obvious choice is to develop a signaling scheme that involves tapping each other's foot. For instance, one tap could signify a lane pass to the five-man, two taps for a wall pass, three taps for a shot opportunity, etc. Whatever scheme is developed, make sure that the signals are easily interpretable, since a perfect pass is useless if it is not caught. Remember that as you work on the mechanics of passing the ball make sure that both you and your teammate pay attention to the footwork. After all, it does take two to tango.

# Part IV

---

# Creating an Unstoppable Offense

# CHAPTER 13

## General Strategies for Offense

Some foosball players might argue that passing is the most important element of foosball, because without a good pass you will never have the opportunity to score. And, some players will argue that defense is the most important part of the game, because a weak defense will surely cost a player the game. While these facets of the game are important, ultimately the game boils down to who can score the most goals. And in order to score proficiently, you need to develop a strong offensive shot.

Learning to develop a good offense involves first learning how to spot an open hole in the defense, then learning the techniques for shooting the ball into the open hole. The first part is easy. In general, there are three zones of the goal that need to be covered, **the pull hole, the middle hole,** and **the push hole.** (Figure 13.1) However, the defender can only cover two of these zones at a time. Learning to spot which hole is open is simply a matter of seeing which zone is not covered. Often, defenders will leave an unusually large pull hole, because from their perspective it seems partially covered.

The next step is to learn how to shoot the ball into the open hole. The following chapters outline some of the most commonly used shots in foosball. As a beginner, your shots will initially lack a great deal of speed, so it is important to learn a shot that enables you to shoot into any open hole from the same starting position. All of the shots presented here have some degree of flexibility for shot making, but some are specifically tailored as **speed shots** designed to beat your opponent in a race to an open hole. These shots are the push shot, pull shot, pass kick, and snake shot. The shots used as **option shots** are the snake shot, back pin shots, and front pin shots. Without a doubt, the two most commonly used shots are the snake shot and the pull shot.

As a beginning player, the snake shot is probably the best shot to learn. It offers the advantages of speed and multiple options. The snake shot will allow you to develop a competitive shot in a short amount of time. As your overall skills begin to develop, you should then learn either the pull shot, push shot, or pass kick. Continue to develop these shots while using the snake shot until they become viable speed-shots. At this point, continue to concentrate on developing one single shot to its fullest potential. Naturally, you should select the one that is the most comfortable for you. Tips for developing your primary shot are given in the tips for advanced player's section of the book. (Chapter 23)

**Figure 13.1** - Illustration of different targets on the goal.

An important point to keep in mind when learning any of the shots is to avoid becoming speed crazy. Do not sacrifice precision for speed. A fast shot is useless if it misses the goal. Always practice at a speed that approaches the limit where you lose control of the shot. You will find that this limit will steadily increase without exerting too much effort. Overexerting yourself will only lead to frustration and strained muscles. So play with control and the speed will develop naturally.

Finally, remember that you are not playing in a vacuum, so pay close attention to the defender. Learn to spot the holes that are left open. And learn to spot any patterns in the defense. This can only be learned through experience. However the more you play, the greater your abilities will become. Just take it one shot at a time and before you know it, the score will read 5-0.

# CHAPTER 14

# The Snake Shot

As one of the most used shots in tournament play, **the snake shot** merits special attention. The speed and fluidity of this shot renders it both elegant and unstoppable; from one position the shooter can potentially hit every open hole. Despite the fact that it is one of the most powerful shots, it is relatively easy to learn. With practice a competitive shot can be developed in under a month, though mastering the shot requires effort and dedication.

Simply, the shot begins with the ball front-pinned in the center of the table. From this position, the offense has the option of hitting the push, pull, or middle hole. (Figure 14.2a) Unlike other shots, the ball is advanced into the goal upon striking it with a counterclockwise rotation of the middle forward. (Figure 14.2b-c)

Once the ball is secured in the front-pin position, you must change your grip. Position your inner wrist such that it cradles the handle. (Figure 14.1 a) From here you are ready to start the shot. In order to first "feel" the shot, do not worry about moving the ball laterally. Concentrate on simply hitting the ball straight. To do this, quickly raise your arm, letting the handle roll down your wrist, into your hand, and catching it hard with your fingers. (Figure 14.2b-c) It is imperative that this rollover is FAST yet terminate in a snapping fashion, resulting in the ball rocketing off of the playing figure.

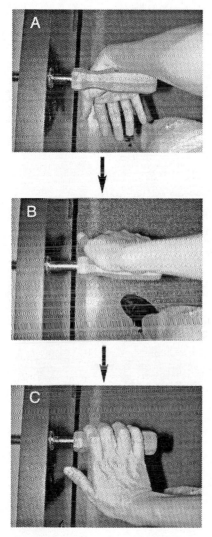

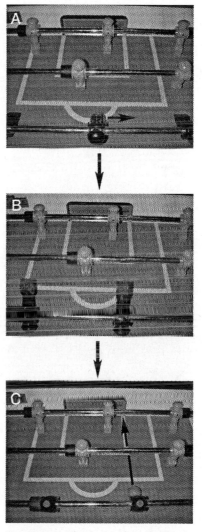

**Figure 14.1** - The Rollover. **A.** The grip begins by cradling the handle in the wrist. **B-C.** To shoot the ball, rotate the hand around the handle and catch it in the fingetips.

**Figure 14.2** - The Snake Shot. **A.** The setup begins with the ball back-pinned on the center three-man. **B-C.** Executing a pull snake shot involves pulling the ball toward the wall, while the figure rotates around to strike it into the goal.

After you feel comfortable with the straight shot, try moving the ball laterally to the push or pull side WITHOUT striking it. Always try to move the ball as fast as possible while still moving it perfectly lateral. If your lateral motion is not consistently fast, you will never win the race against your opponent.

The culmination of your practice comes when you combine the two motions into one flowing shot. Begin by rolling, pausing, and then shooting the ball. Though slow at first, the pause time will decrease with continual practice and the three motions will quickly blend into one powerful shot. Eventually, the shot will feel effortlessly natural.

After having developed the mechanics of the shot, you will want to begin optimizing its use. An important technique is the **rattle**. From the starting position, rock the ball from side to side while maintaining constant contact between the ball and the middle forward. This action will increase your feel for how the ball will roll. When you are ready to shoot, explode to one side and smoke it into the goal. In addition, varying your stance can improve the performance of your shot. Especially in doubles play, make sure your partner is leaving you enough room for you to take a comfortable stance. Also, with continual practice, you should experience a whip-like feel to the shot. This is a result of the shoulder moving in the direction opposite of the shot. To perfect a truly devastating shot, it is important to pay close attention to developing this recoiling action.

Now, your snake is ready to inject its venom.

# CHAPTER 15

# The Push and Pull Shots

Sometimes the best things in life are the simplest. The push and pull shots are no exception. These shots are the easiest to learn because they require the fewest movements. Yet, their simplicity should by no means reflect the caliber of the shot. In spite of its rather basic stroke, or perhaps because of it, the shot remains one of the most popular in the foosball arena. As a first offensive shot to learn, it is perhaps one of the best candidates.

The **push shot** and **pull shot** are symmetric shots, with the push developing away from you and the pull developing toward you. The **pull shot** begins with the three-man rod pushed against the opposite wall and the ball sitting on the inside of the middle three-man. (Figure 15.1a) Your opponent will most likely have his defenders directly in front of you. The object is to move the ball around these defenders and shoot the ball into the open goal with the center three-man. Set the ball in motion by pulling the rod toward you. Next, raise the middle figure and position him behind the ball in order to prepare for the wrist flick to shoot the ball. (Figure 15.1b) By the time the ball is past the defenders, you should have the middle three-man centered behind the ball. (Figure 15.1c) Just snap the wrist to send the ball into the open goal. When you have mastered the shot, it will feel like a fluid, whip-like motion and the ball is always in contact with the center three-man. The ball clings desperately to the playing figure before being launched into oblivion. **The push shot** proceeds in the same manner, except in the opposite direction, away from you.

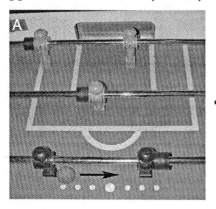

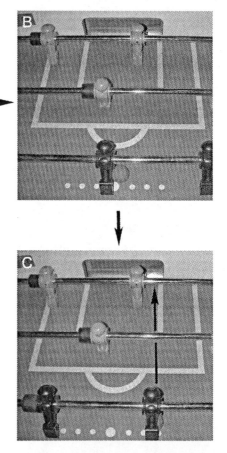

Figure 15.1 - The Pull Shot. **A.** The ball is setup on the inside of the middle three-man near the far side of the goal. The ball is set in motion by pulling the ball toward the wall. **B.** The middle three-man moves behind the ball as it is rolling. **C.** And finally, the middle-three man strikes the ball into the goal. The push shot is executed in the same way, except the ball starts on the near side of the goal and is pushed to the far side of the goal.

There are a few points worth noting. Remember to start with the three-man rod as close as possible to the edge of the goal, since that position will leave you with more space on the goal. If the ball starts in front of the middle of the goal, there will be little space remaining between the defenders and the edge of the goal. Of course, if your opponent chooses not to cover the goal directly in front of you, don't waste your going around him, just SHOOT! When working with both the push and the pull, you may find that one shot feels more natural than the other. This phenomenon is common, use your best as your "big gun".

Remember that the idea behind the shot entails beating the defender with the use of sheer speed. When your opponent presents you with a stationary defense, you must race around his men to put the ball in the goal. In the event he adopts a moving defense, you must still rely heavily on speed while picking a hole between his men. As you develop this shot, you will gain a feel for how long it takes to move and shoot the ball into a hole. This will greatly help in shooting on a moving defense, since you will have a "sixth" sense about whether or not you will have time to place the ball in a hole that suddenly opens in the defense.

With practice, the push and pull should quickly become one of your favorite shots.

# CHAPTER 16

# The Pass Kick

Once you are comfortable with the basic push and pull shots, you can proceed to add options to your repertoire. A good candidate is **the pass kick**. The motions are simple, as in the push and pull shots, but timing and coordination now become more critical.

As with the push and pull shots, **the pass kick** can develop in either direction—away or towards the shooter. The following explanation describes a shot that moves away from the shooter. Keep in mind that the exact same steps may be used in the reverse direction. The shot begins with the ball resting against the inside of the three-man closest to you. (Figure 16.1a) Push the rod away to set the ball in motion. As the ball crosses in front of the goal, hit it with the center three-man in to the goal. (Figure 16.1b) With this shot you have the option of where in the goal you want to shoot. As the ball moves across the front of the goal, you can hit it with the three-man at any point in front of the near side of the goal, in the middle, or on the far side.

A nice shot to work in tandem with the pass kick is the **angle shot**. The shot begins from the same position as the pass kick. However, instead of moving the ball in front of the goal and shooting with the center three-man, shoot the ball with the outer man resting next to the ball. After you start moving the ball with the outer man, angle it into the near corner of the goal. (Figure 16.1c) Because the pass kick and the angle shot have the same setup, your opponent will not know which shot is coming next. They will be forced to either guard the near corner against the angle or protect the middle and far corners against the pass kick. Maintaining a good mix between the two shots will keep your opponent off-guard.

Keep practicing the pass kick, and you're guaranteed to leave the defense guessing.

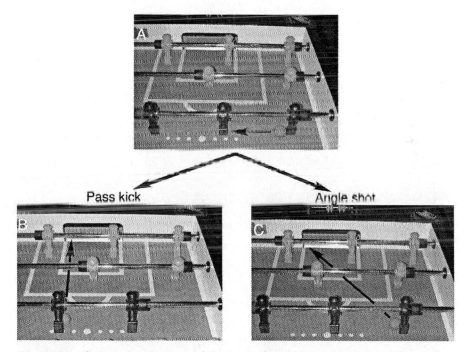

**Figure 16.1** - The Pass Kick Series. **A.** The setup for the push pass kick begins with the ball on the inside of the first three-man. The ball is passed to the middle three-man by pushing the rod toward the far wall. **B.** The pass kick is completed when the middle three-man shoots the ball into the far side of the goal. **C.** Alternatively, if there is a gap in the defense, the ball can be angled into the goal by striking the ball off-center.

# CHAPTER 17

## The Back-Pin Series

Although speed and accuracy are important factors in developing a stunning offensive shot, most beginning players usually lack this level of skill. Consequently, most shots will end up either stopped by the goalie or wide of the goal. These difficulties can often be overcome with sufficient practice; however, the beginning player could benefit from having a wide variety of shots in order to confuse and disorient the defender. Not only is it important to have a wide variety of shots, but it is more important that the defender is unable to anticipate which shot is coming from a given setup.

It is in this respect that the **back-pin series** is especially useful. Like the snake shot and front pin series, it uses one position to initiate a wide variety of shots. However, unlike these two, all shots in this series start from having the ball back-pinned in the center position. (Figure 17.1a) The fundamental shots from this position are the back-pin-push and back-pin-pull shots. The execution of both shots is essentially equivalent with the exception that the ball is moved in different directions.

The **back-pin-pull** is executed by initially placing a slight downward pressure on the ball followed by pulling the rod towards the body. The ball will begin to travel on a slightly angled path towards the near wall. As it does so, position the center three-man on a line perpendicular to the near-edge of the goal. Wait until the ball comes into striking range, and hit the near half of the ball in order to counteract the ball's lateral motion. This should result in the ball traveling on a straight path towards the goal. (Figure 17.1b) Note: striking the ball on the far-edge will result in the ball **spraying** wide of the goal since additional lateral momentum is added.

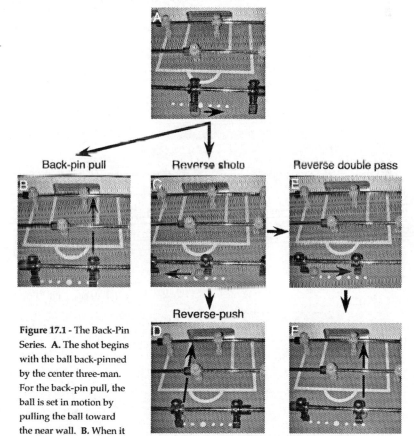

**Figure 17.1** - The Back-Pin Series. **A.** The shot begins with the ball back-pinned by the center three-man. For the back-pin pull, the ball is set in motion by pulling the ball toward the near wall. **B.** When it is aligned with the near side of the goal, the center three-man strikes it. **C.** Alternatively, the ball can be reversed towards the far hole by bringing the center three-man to the side of the ball and then pushing it toward the opposite wall. **D.** When it reaches the far side, the center strikes it into the goal. **E.** As another option from C, the ball can be passed yet by the far three-man back to the center three-man. **F.** When it reaches the near side of the goal, the center three-man strikes it into the goal.

The **back-pin-push** is executed in the opposite fashion, i.e. the ball is pushed towards the far wall and the ball is struck on the far edge of the ball. As you practice these shots and become more adept, the individual shots should blend and become less defined. It is important to develop this degree of comfort before attempting the slightly more advanced shots in the series.

The ultimate strength of the backpin series lies in the ability to "fake out" your opponent by quickly changing the traveling direction of the ball. Such shots are called **reverses**. The **reverse push**, for instance, is initiated in the same way as a back-pin-pull, i.e. by applying a downward stroking motion toward the near wall. Now, instead of setting the center three-man up for a shot on the near side of the goal, move the center three-man along the direction of the incoming ball and slow the ball down slightly by following it along the direction of travel. Quickly, before the ball stops, execute a standard push shot to the far side of the goal. (Figure 17.1c-d) Similarly, a **reverse-pull** is executed by starting as a back-pin-push and reversing into a pull shot to the near side goal. Some players find it easier to simply "roll" the playing figure around the side of the ball and then execute the push. However, this motion often gives away the intent of the shot.

If you begin to find that the reverse is anticipated, the direction of the ball can be altered again by executing a pass-kick with the outside playing figure back to the center figure. In fact, this is a **double-pass kick** since the ball is passed from the outside figure and then passed back to the center playing figure. For example, the **reverse-push-double-pass kick** starts like a reverse; but instead of pushing the ball, pass the ball to the far-side three-man then pass it back to the center three-man and finally hit it into the goal. (Figure 17.1 e-f) Of course, you can pass between your men indefinitely, but the shot is less effective at deceiving your opponent with each pass.

Finally, you must always be mindful of a defender leaving an open middle hole. If this persists, subtly move the ball into a back-pin position such that it will easily slip out. Then, quickly shoot the ball forward into the goal. The trick is of course to make it appear as if the ball is in a tight back-pin. Like all of the other shots in the series, this requires a good deal of timing, fluidity, and gamesmanship to pull off successfully. But, with attention to the finer points of the series, you should easily have the defender guessing.

# CHAPTER 18

## The Front-Pin Series

As mentioned in the previous chapter, players who are unable to generate sufficient speed and power need shots with several options. Here, the **front-pin series** of shots have several of the same advantages as the back-pin series with some minor tradeoffs.

As the name implies, all of the shots in the series start with the ball front-pinned in the center position. (Figure 18.1a) The basic options from this position are the **front-pin-pull** and the **front-pin-push**. These maneuvers are slightly more complicated than the corresponding back-pin shots. As an example, the **front-pin-pull** starts by applying a slight downward pressure to the pinned ball. Next, pull the figure towards the near wall. Circle the figure around such that it winds up on a line behind the ball. Once the man is lined up with the near-edge of the goal, strike the ball into the goal. (Figure 18.1b) The **front-pin-push** can be executed in the reverse fashion by moving towards the far wall.

In addition, many of the same reversing techniques can be accomplished with the front-pin series. The reverse series is initiated in the same manner as the front-pin pull, but instead of swinging the middle three-man behind the ball, the figure is swung in line of the oncoming ball. From here, a push, a pass-kick, or a double-pass-kick can be executed. (Figure 18.1c-e)

One of the drawbacks of the front-pin series is that the push and pull take longer to execute, since the three-man has to swing behind the ball in order to strike it. Granted, in the hands of an expert, the difference may be a few milliseconds, but even that can make a difference against a strong defense.

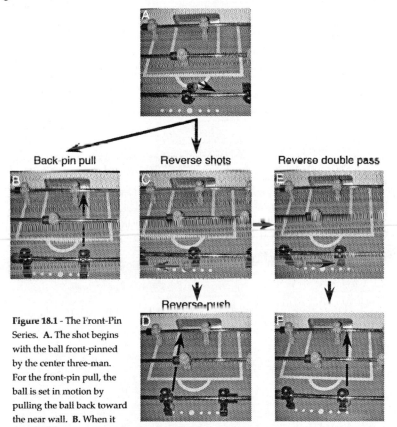

**Figure 18.1** - The Front-Pin Series. **A.** The shot begins with the ball front-pinned by the center three-man. For the front-pin pull, the ball is set in motion by pulling the ball back toward the near wall. **B.** When it is aligned with the near side of the goal, the center three-man strikes it. **C.** Alternatively, the ball can be reversed towards the far hole by bringing the center three-man to the side of the ball and then pushing it toward the opposite wall. **D.** When it reaches the far side, the center strikes it into the goal. **E.** As another option from C, the ball can be passed yet by the far three-man back to the center three-man. **F.** When it reaches the near side of the goal, the center three-man strikes it into the goal. This series is similar to the Back-Pin Series, however it starts from a front-pin instead of a back-pin.

Most players are not inclined to use the front-pin series for that reason. As explained in the previous chapter, the back-pin series confers all of the same advantages as the front-pin series, but with the additional advantage that it is fundamentally faster. So, why learn the front-pin series? Despite the drawbacks, the front-pin series is still useful in catching your opponent off guard.

Used in conjunction with the snake shot, the front-pin can be especially devastating. Since the snake shot begins with the ball front-pinned, the initial setup is indistinguishable except for the fact that a grip change is required to use the snake shot. If you are using the snake shot and sense that your opponent is relaxing during the grip-change, then this is the perfect time to quickly execute a front-pin-push or front-pin-pull.

Similarly, if you constantly use the back-pin series and take the time to maneuver your ball from a front-pin to a back-pin, your opponent may be relaxing during this interval. Once again, this is the time to quickly execute a front-pin-push or front-pin-pull.

One final situation that occurs frequently is in passing the ball. Usually, the ball will end up trapped in a front-pin. If the situation is right, a quick front-pin shot can score a quick extra point.

In summary, the front-pin series is a good source of secondary shots. It is important to have a wide variety of these secondary shots in addition to your main shot when developing your offense. As you begin to improve your main shot, you may not have to rely on catching your opponent off-guard with improvised tricks. Still, it is important not to forget these little shots, because when the game is on the line, anything goes.

# Part V

---

# Building an Impenetrable Defense

# CHAPTER 19

## The Role of Defense

Defense in foosball involves stopping, catching, hitting, or deflecting any ball that was last hit by one of your opponent's figures. Besides blocking the opponent's shots on your goal, you will also need to regain control of the ball after it bounces in your area so that you may then pass the ball to your offense or even take a shot at your opponent's goal. Yes, passing and shooting from the defense are also an integral part of the game.

Always bear in mind that the object of defensive play is to prevent the opponent from scoring. It is especially important for the beginner to understand this. It is okay to accidentally knock the ball into your own goal while on defense. When an experienced player suffers an **own-goal**, he merely bows his head, gets the next ball in play, slaps it to his offense, and he or his partner summarily shoot it into the opponent's goal. So don't worry about scoring an own-goal.

The beginning player should feel right at home on defense. There, he controls the one portion of the table that gives him the most space to practice ball control, to set up new shots, to taunt the opponent with idle tapping and passing, or simply to catch a breather. Think of being on defense as commanding your own playground.

So, with the right mindset, let us begin with the stance. Stand a little way behind the goalie, grip the goalie rod with the left hand and the two-man rod with the right, and keep your body tilted towards the opponent's goal. Stay a reasonable distance away from the table so that you can comfortably push the rods all the way to the far wall as well as pull them all the way to the near wall. Be sure to maintain a comfortable stance with your weight on one foot, body leaning forward, and the other foot back but firmly on the floor. But, don't be like a statue in Central Park! A proper stance allows you flexibility to move your body in time with your mental reaction. When you need to move, move! And remember the important role that you are playing on defense!

# CHAPTER 20

## Defensive Strategies

In this chapter, we will consider different defensive strategies. First, you should learn to set up a basic **line-up**. These line-ups alternate between two different positions. In the first position, place the goalie and one figure from the two-man rod a ball's width apart. Tilt both figures so that their feet are close together but not so much that the ball can slip under the playing figure. (Figure 20.1a) Adjust your grip so that your wrists are relaxed. Now from this position, rotate both the goalie and the two-man rod counterclockwise so that the defenders seem to be sliding into the opponents. Once again, take care not to lift the men too high off the table thereby leaving a wide-open space for the ball to slip by into the goal.

Note: It is important to adjust the space between the goalie and the closest defender according to the play. Give more that a ball's width if the opponent seems unable or unwilling to shoot at the middle of the goal. Give less than a ball's width if the opponent seems to be shooting for the space between your defenders. In other words, a widely spaced defense is best for covering the sides of the goal, and a tightly spaced defense is best for covering the middle of the goal.

Keeping the figures' feet tilted towards each other will close a middle gap through which the ball may pass into the goal if shot at an angle.

This also affords the best formation from which to regain control of the ball after it rebounds in your area.

With this basic line-up, you are now ready to put into play one of many strategies for defending the goal. Perhaps the easiest strategy to consider is a **race defense**. Treat your defensive line-up (goalie and closest defender) as one unit. Move them as one. Whether fast or slow, smooth or sudden, move the defense as one. Push or pull the rods synchronously so that the gap between your defenders never changes. Keep the defense directly in front of the ball when it is being handled anywhere in front of the goal. When the ball is moved off to one side, place the defensive line-up such that the closest figure is directly in the line-of-fire between the ball and the goal's corner. As long as you maintain the correct defensive position with respect to the ball's location, the opponent can not score. You will always be blocking his direct line of fire and he will need to move the ball around you when he shoots. When he shoots, you need to race your defensive line-up to block the ball. (Figure 20.1b)

Try to follow the ball, not the man. Make sure not to overstep your goal area. Your defensive line-up is useless when it's blocking the wall. Finally, try not to jump at every moment. The opponent may try to "fake you out" by shooting straight ahead while hoping for you to jump out of the way.

Another style of defense, known as **steady one and blast two**, is good if you are much faster moving only a single rod. When the opponent sets up his shot, position your defensive line-up as you would in a race defense. When he shoots, move only one rod to block the shot while leaving the other steady.

Another defense strategy takes a more proactive approach to guarding the goal. Rather than waiting for your opponent to shoot and then racing to block the hole, the defender attempts to bait the shooter for a specific hole and then quickly blocks it. This style of defense is usually good when your opponent is slow in setting up shots and favors shooting to a particular side of the goal. It is also useful when you want to force your opponent to make shots on one side of the goal only. This may be because your opponent has a weak side or you are quicker racing to that side.

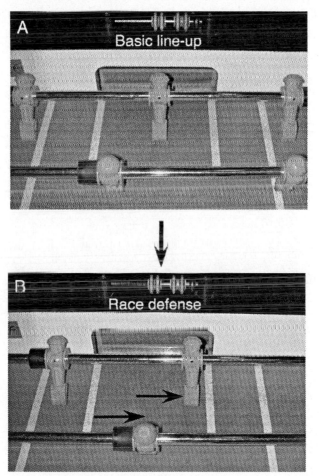

**Figure 20.1 - A.** The basic line-up is setup by placing the near two-man closest to the push hole and the center goalie near the middle hole. **B.** The race defense relies on swiftly moving both figures to cover the open hole.

By keeping your defensive line-up offset from his direct line-of-fire, you make it easier and therefore more tempting for the opponent to shoot on the open side. Therefore, you can better anticipate his shots and gain a small margin when racing to block his shots. However, don't always expect your opponent to go for the bait. Remember to follow the ball. Finally, take care not to offset your defensive line-up so that it no longer blocks the direct shot on goal.

These strategies should give you the foundation on which to build an impenetrable defense.

# CHAPTER 21

## Shots from Defense

Getting set to make a shot from defense involves being ready from the moment the ball enters the goal area. When the ball rebounds in your goal area, try to regain control of it so that you can either pass it to your offense or make a shot from the defense. Tilt the feet of your defenders out front while sweeping the rod over to stop the ball from escaping your reach. Once the ball knocks behind a defender, pull it back into your area with a smooth lateral sweep of the two-man rod while rotating the defenders inwards.

Now, you're ready to take a shot. First, spot and aim for an opening in your opponent's goal. Then, find a clear path to the goal. Finding the open holes in the opponent's defense is a seemingly impossible task for the beginner. Nevertheless, it is one of the easiest skills to acquire.

Choose your target, either an open space in the opposing goal or a spot where you anticipate an opening. In the beginning, it is best to choose a space that is already open. Once your shot is fast enough, you will score. Next, pick a gateway in the opponent's three-man barrier. Now, look at the straight path from the gate in the three-man to the target of the opposing goal. If one of your opponent's five-men is directly in your path, then there is no hole and that path is blocked. Look to a different target or different spaces in the three-man. If you can envision a straight line that isn't broken by the five-man figure then you have a clear path to the goal.

When learning, it is helpful to stand directly behind your goal and to look down the table to see if you can spot the holes and open paths. Then, after noting the shot trajectory, return to the defensive position to observe what the arrangement looks like from the player's angle. (Figure 21.1a) Once you have spotted a clear path to the goal, you may choose any type of shot that you have learned. Position the ball appropriately relative to the hole and make the shot.

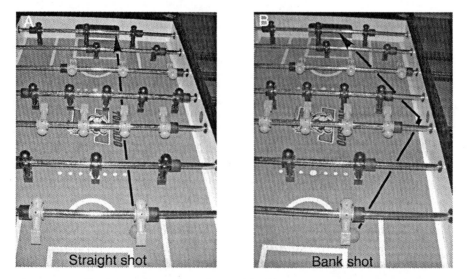

**Figure 21.1** - Shots from defense. **A.** The straight shot is accomplished when there is a straight gateway to the goal. **B.** Alternatively, a bank shot will also work. The ball must be contacted off-center in order for the ball to travel on the appropriate trajectory. For both shots, it is important to remember to lift your three-man and five-man rods so that the ball can travel underneath them.

Never fear if you don't see an open straight shot to the goal, you also have the option of a **bank shot**. To execute a bank shot, kick the ball swiftly and slightly off-center as if you are kicking with the edge of the playing figure. The ball should accelerate powerfully at an angle, bank off the side of the table and rocket into the goal. (Figure 21.1b) With practice, you will be able to fine-tune the initial angle as well as the overall trajectory of the shot. Start by getting the ball in a backpin, then adjusting the position until the ball slips out at an angle. This gives you an idea of where you have to hit the ball. The bank is a great shot to make from the defense. This is simply because the angle that the ball needs to travel is usually less than 45-degrees and is much easier to execute.

So now you have what it takes to make great shots from the defense. You'll have fun impressing yourself and your friends by accomplishing the seemingly impossible.

# CHAPTER 22

# Forward Defense

In general, one usually associates the forward position with the offense. Although offense is the forward player's main job, part of the time must be spent acting in a defensive role. The forward player must contend with a large array of attacks and passes from the defense. Countering these attacks is also a job for the forward player. Luckily, a wide array of defensive tactics can be used to counter these attacks.

Perhaps the most important concern for the forward player is to prevent a shot by the opposing team's defense. Nothing can change the momentum of a game faster than a well executed shot by the defense. The forward player must especially guard against the straight shot and bank shot by the opposing team's defense. The best strategy for guarding against both of these shots is to first set your defense to guard the opponent's pull and middle hole. (Figure 22.1) Of course, this is not to say that your defense is glued to this position, but it simplifies your task in the forward position to only guard the push hole. In addition, the opponent's line of sight to the push hole is much worse than to the pull hole. By forcing your opponent into shooting for this hole, you have reduced his shot options considerably. However, the defense also has the option of executing passes to his five-man or three-man. Consequently, the forward player is left to guard a straight shot, bank shot, straight pass, or push pass. All of which start from essentially the same position and are thus initially indistinguishable.

There are essentially three line-ups for your five-man and three-man rod that can block these options. In the first line-up, your closest three-man guards the straight shot while your five-man guards the bank shot against the near wall. However, a push pass to the near wall is left open. (Figure 22.1a) The second position is essentially a transition setup in which the near three-man is blocking the bank shot while the five-man is guarding the straight shot. This, however, leaves both pass options open. (Figure 22.1b) The final position has the three-man guarding the push pass and the the straight shot, but leaves the bank shot open. (Figure 22.1c)

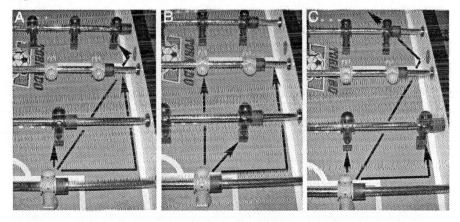

**Figure 22.1** - Forward defense. Three defensive line-ups are illustrated using the offensive three-man and five-man rods. **A.** The first line-up blocks the straight shot and bank shot, but it leaves the push pass open. **B.** The second line-up blocks the bank, but it leaves the passes open. **C.** The final line-up blocks the passes, but it leaves the bank shot open. Switching between these line-ups is an important part of defending from the offensive rods.

So, how should you use these line-ups to block all of the possible shots? Well, it depends on the situation. If your opponent appears to be a poor bank shooter, you can spend less time guarding that shot. Similarly, if he has an excellent push pass, you may wish to spend more time guarding the wall. Of course, if he seems to be an all around good player, you can use a **stochastic defense** (randomized movement) or a **bait defense** (exposing a hole and quickly blocking it). As you can see, defense from the forward position requires the same degree of concentration as playing straight defense.

The same is true for guarding passes from the five-man to the three-man. In general, the passes will be headed for the wall or the lane, and you must spend time guarding both the wall and lane. Initially, you can try to simply stay in front of the ball at all times; however, this strategy quickly breaks down against fast passes, and the brush pass. Once again, pay attention to which pass your opponent prefers. And if he is an all-around good passer, try baiting or a stochastic defense.

Finally, one has to be on the look out for random shots by the defense. There usually is no way to anticipate these shots, but being ready for them might give you an edge in gaining possession of a randomly struck ball. It is unlikely that your opponent will attempt a random shot from the five-man, since it will most likely wind up in your possession on defense. In which case, it will be your opponent's turn on forward defense.

Part VI

# When the Unstoppable Force Meets the Impenetrable Object: Techniques for Advanced Play

# CHAPTER 23

## Stepping up the Offense

Okay, so now you think you're hot stuff just because you've mastered all of the shots mentioned in the previous chapters. But what are you going to do when you come up against Big Bad Bubba on defense?! Hey, just because you feel like you can take on the world with that shot you've been practicing on your buddy Earl, doesn't mean that you can execute when the game is on the line. So, what makes you think that Big Bad Bubba will be afraid of your puny shot? Well, he will be if you step up your level of play. Boom Shaka Laka. So, the first thing you will need to do is keep your cool. Bubba may be Big, but he's not all that Bad.

So, how do we keep Bubba off guard? Well, there are two key elements that make an offensive shot great. These are SPEED, POWER, ACCURACY, TEMPO, UNPREDICTABILITY and CONTROL. Okay, so technically that's six areas, but what are you going to do about it, punk? I'll tell you what. You're going to stop wasting time practicing with Earl and improve these five areas. Let's consider each individually, shall we?

SPEED. If there is one thing that Bubba will respect, it's a fast shot. And, by far this is what most players strive to achieve in their daily practice. But, we all know the guys who want to be like Freddy Fast and Loose, with his cool jet-black hair and his devil may care attitude. But, try to go too fast—too soon and you'll wind up like a Sammy Spray and Play, who shoots it fast but whose ball winds up in no man's land. So, the key to picking up speed without losing control is PATIENCE. Don't go from 0 to 100 mph in one practice session. Incrementally increase your speed to the point where you begin to lose control. This is the level that you need to practice the shot at for that particular session. At the next session, it will feel like your shot has risen from the dead, because you will find that the troublesome speed is now trivial.

POWER. Bubba could care less for a fast shot with no power behind it. So now that you're fast, can you deliver the ball with force? Can you get the ball into the goal with enough cahoneys to make your opponent squeal like a little pig? Well, if you can't, then you will, once you've strengthened your wrist flick. There are several exercises for developing the muscles in your wrist. Most players utilize what is known as a putty ball that strengthens the wrist muscles through a set of squeezing exercises. But, the top players use fingertip push-ups which develops all of the hand, wrist, and arm muscles. Start with the putty ball, then work your way up to the finger tip push-ups. You'll have Bubba squealing in no time.

ACCURACY. Bubba is a sucker for a well placed shot. So, once you've started drilling those shots, you need to make sure that they're actually hitting the goal. If you're not, you'll be just like a Tommy Too-Wide who people would play, but would never defend against. Say, "Bye. Bye. Tommy Too-Wide," and, "Hello, Slick Straight-and-Good". The only drill for developing accuracy is the dead-man drill. Put the opposing two-man rod dead against the wall, and shoot around it. Can't do it, Tommy? Well, try starting with the playing figure two-fingers off the wall, and slowly move it in as you get better. (Figure 23.1) Whoa! Watch it, Slick! You're on your way to the top now!

TEMPO. To keep Bubba off guard you should make sure that you vary the tempo of your shots. What do we mean by tempo? Well, you should try to vary the time spent on setting up the shot, in addition to

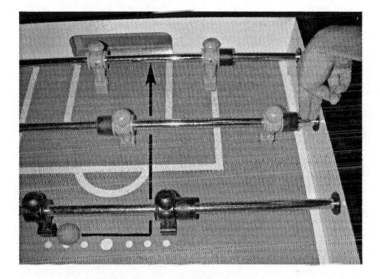

**Figure 23.1** - Two-finger drill. For practicing shots to the pull or push holes, position the two-man rod such that the spacer is two-finger lengths off of the wall. This will leave a small space to shoot around the far two-man. As you get better, try a one-finger drill. Then, try a dead-man drill, i.e. the spacer is flush against the wall.

varying the point at which you actually take the shot. We all tend to fall into patterns, which a good defender may pick up on. But if you remain conscious of when you are taking the shot, you can ensure that you are not presenting a predictable offense. Not only will varying the timing of the shot help your offense, but also implementing a wide variety of shots will keep Bubba off guard. You may even consider taking a shot when you are in the middle of setting up. Bubba will not be paying attention when you are "setting up," and so you can just go ahead and shoot. BAM! BUBBA! BAM! Along these same lines, never be afraid to experiment with your shots. Bubba may not be ready for something he has never seen before. So go ahead and take those wacky and wild shots. Remember to bring the tempo of the game to your level and to what you want.

UNPREDICTABILITY. If you can confuse Bubba, you can lose Bubba. There are two keys to maintaining unpredictability and using the element of surprise when on the offense: fluid grace and varying tempo. If you always move the ball smoothly such that the man seems to only keep light contact with the ball, your opponent will find that your shots become indistinguishable from your passes until it is too late. Keep close to the ball. Don't lift the man too far off of the ball when passing or shooting. Backing off of the ball makes passing and shooting jerky and uncomfortable, and leads to a weak and predictable game. Keep close to the ball and follow through on the pass or shot. Try taking shots quickly. Slowly setup and then accelerate into the shot. Or, without any setup, whack the ball towards the goal if you see a space. Also, change your setup a few times. Or you can move the ball from one side of the table to the next, make passes instead of shots, or even fake a shot. Do whatever it takes to avoid falling into a pattern that Bubba can read. Bubba may be slow, but he can tell a pattern from a hole in the ground.

CONTROL. If you can take control of the game, Bubba will be putty in your hands. When making a shot, concentrate on executing the shot. Do not be daunted or distracted by the defense. Always play the shot and not the defense. Beforehand, you would have observed the defense and have decided on what shot you want to make. For the moment, when you actually execute the shot, you should forget about what the defense is thinking and concentrate on making the shot the way you want to make it. Play the shot not the defense. This will help you improve your shooting precision. Concentrate on getting your shot off smoothly and beating the defense will come naturally. You will be able to gain a feel for your shots and will be able to tune your motions to achieve the speed and trajectory you intend. Often times, one is not focused on how he is making the shot because he is trying to adjust for what he thinks the defense is doing while making the shot. This only causes one to lose control of the shot and eventually the game.

Keep these pointers in mind and you'll have Bubba telling all of his cell buddies about your unstoppable offense.

# CHAPTER 24

## Strengthening the Defense

After Bubba has had that little talk with his cellmates, you will need to spend some extra time strengthening your defense. So now you have a problem. Big Bad Bubba is no longer on defense; he's on offense, and it's your job to stop him. And you can bet that he has learned all your advanced offensive techniques and will be trying them against you. The first thing to remember is that foosball is mostly an offensive game. Having a good defense is a challenge, an art, and a religion. Only a few people can truly master the defense. Can you be one of them? Well if you've purchased our book, sure, you can at least think you're one of them. But, I digress. The key to the impenetrable defense is realizing that it is really a mind game. Can you confuse Bubba enough so that his focus is drawn away from his completing the shot and drawn instead to contemplating your defense? If you can accomplish this, you have already blocked the shot. You have stolen his "chi". It is no longer within his shot, but rather within your defense. So your task has been simplified to simply drawing his attention away from his shot to your defense instead. The best way to achieve this goal is to make sure your defense is truly random and chaotic. Make sure you don't fall into a pattern. You can also "psyche him out" by occasionally leaving big "holes" in the defense and then suddenly closing up these holes. Bait him! Bubba is no more than a big dumb fish. Just think of your task as trying to hook a 300-pound hardened criminal. There's nothing like a little good bayou fishing.

Try to confuse Bubba by switching the relative positions of the goalie and the closest defender so that the goalie is either inside or outside the space between the two figures of the two-man rod. You may also switch the defensive line-up by switching the "chosen" defender of the two-man rod so that either the far-side defender or near-side defender is used in conjunction with the goalie to form the defensive line-up. Alternating the defensive line-up in these ways is guaranteed to confuse Bubba and make him lose his concentration. When making a switch, be sure to keep at least one man in front of the ball. Note, as the opponent moves the ball from one side to the other, it is best to switch the defensive line-up such that the two-man defender of the defensive lineup is covering the middle of the goal, the goalie is covering the corner nearest the ball, and the goalie is inside the space between the two defenders.

Following the above guidelines, you will create a powerful defensive style, but you may still be predictable. When you believe that being unpredictable will be more advantageous than having graceful form, switch back to the random defense. Switch your defensive line-up quickly, wildly, and randomly. Tilt the line-up forward, tilt the line-up back, stop in front of the ball a moment, and then switch the line-up again. Follow no pattern—no guidelines, except do not overshoot the goal too often.

Also, keep in mind that your job as defender is two-fold. Not only do you have to block Bubba's shots, you must also clear the ball to the offense or make a shot on goal yourself. As always you want to keep Bubba guessing which option you will take. So a good strategy to follow is to set the ball alongside one of the figures on the two-man rod. Now, tap the ball from one figure to the next so that the ball hits directly into the side of the adjacent figure and bounces exactly the way it came, back to the first figure. Try to keep tapping the ball back and forth from one man to the next for as long as you can. Try to achieve a tap-tap rhythm where you keep the ball moving back and forth in a steady straight-line path using short, swift lateral knocks. As a cultural note, the Spaniards have developed this drill into an actual shot, where they start tapping the ball from side to side and then Slam! They either pass or shoot the ball into the goal. Expect to see this maneuver often if you happen to be playing on tables in Madrid.

Once the timing is right, this maneuver is most effective. Indeed, the drill is to build up one's timing as well as ball control. Vary the drill by choosing a different pair of figures, or by changing the tempo; try to speed up the rhythm, try to slow it down, try to stop and catch the ball, try to chew bubble-gum and walk. You will begin to see your reflexes quicken and your ball control skills improve. This style is wild and fast and can be a great deal of fun.

Finally, keep in mind that many of these techniques can easily be applied to playing the offense. And, many of the techniques learned in offense also apply to the defense. Thus, we see that learning foosball echoes the Taoist philosophy…that things are neither one nor another, offense or defense…they just are. Ponder the essence of being the next time Bubba has stolen your chi on defense.

# CHAPTER 25

# Practice, Practice, Practice

Okay, so you've learned the key elements that make for a superlative offense and a stellar defense, but like most players you're having trouble transforming your knowledge into action. Hey, we all know that the only way to turn knowledge into action is by practicing. So, let's face it. It's the only way to get good at the game. You need to practice and you need to enjoy practicing. There are times when it will become frustrating, but as mentioned elsewhere, when you seem to be stuck in a slump, change your focus. Put yourself in new playing situations. Above all, keep trying. Now, of course, you don't get an 'A' just for effort, but don't be discouraged. Here you will find drills to effectively improve your game as well as remind you of the enjoyment that may be derived by playing the game. But bear in mind that, as the saying goes, "Only perfect practice makes perfect." That is to say, it is possible to practice a bad shot, and become quite adept at flawlessly executing that bad shot. Consequently, paying attention to the key points developed in the previous chapters when you practice is extremely important, otherwise you may become the lord of the lousy shot.

Nevertheless, if you've progressed to this level, it is perhaps safe to say that you have developed a good practice routine. You have undoubtedly accumulated a repertoire of shots and defensive maneuvers that you are able to execute a percentage of the time with pinpoint accuracy. But, if you are like most players, there will quickly come a point in time when constantly practicing appears to yield little results. This is perhaps most disconcerting to the advanced player who begins to feel that there's no room left for improvement.

As you practice your shots, you will discover that you encounter a period when you are able to learn and improve very rapidly. But, as you continue to practice the shots, you will find that you approach a plateau in which no matter how much you continue to practice, you simply can not seem to get any better. In fact, you may observe the somewhat paradoxical result that the more you practice, the WORSE you appear to get! Yowza! If this is happening, don't worry. In fact, this trend is well documented. It is known as the learning curve, (Figure 25.1a) and most people learn new tasks in accordance with the curve.

In simple parlance, it's a rut. And no matter how you slice it, getting out of a rut can be difficult. So, how do you break out of a slump like the one described? Well, as the learning curve would suggest, if you can attempt to make the experience new, then you should find yourself situated at the bottom of a new learning curve that builds on the first one. (Figure 25.1b). Clearly, this is easier said than done.

So, how do you move your game to the next level? One way is by inspecting your practicing behavior. Ask yourself, how often do you practice a shot using the same routine? How many times do you practice your weak shots? How often do you aim for your weak side? How often do you aim for a particular hole when practicing? Chances are that if you're like most players, you tend to practice only what you're good at, and spend little if any time practicing your weak shots. And then, when it comes time to utilize the weak shot, players wonder why they are unable to execute properly! Incredible!

This behavior is not restricted to beginners. A fellow on the professional tour, we'll call Rusty Bottoms, was unable to consistently hit specific holes with his pull shot. The problem: he practiced the shot without goalie figures blocking, because he liked the sound of the ball hitting the goal unimpeded! Admittedly, this is an extreme case, but many of us fall into this type of behavior to some extent.

So, how do we rectify the situation? Well, obviously, changing your practicing routine is the best route. Try to practice shots that you aren't good at. For the shots that seem to have leveled off, try changing the defense you are playing against. Sometimes a minor change can make all the difference. The most important aspect is creating a challenge and keeping yourself entertained while practicing. This type of attention will bring your practice into the new learning curve.

A good drill is a game of beating records. That is, try to make a certain number of shots in a row. Then, try to beat that record. If you miss a shot, start counting over from the beginning. Don't fudge figures! If you miss, start over. This can really become challenging physically as well as mentally as the number of shots increases. It's also very good for teaching you how to handle pressure, especially when you're attempting the shot that will break your old record.

Well, suppose that you have practiced your little heart out, and you still can't get past the guy on defense. You realize that there must be an open hole…somewhere. However, for the life of you, your shots can't seem to find the hole. So, how do you get around the defense? The most common problem in this case is that you are unconsciously telegraphing your shot. At this point in a game, you will find that your best bet is to carefully analyze your movements and see if indeed you are telegraphing. If so, you can use this to your advantage. As an example, a player on the tour, we'll call Telem Marconi, would trick his opponents by letting out a little squeal before executing a weak pull shot. Then, when the opponent was lulled into the pattern, Marconi would squeal like a pig and shoot the opposite push shot for the score. Once again, this is an extreme example, but it illustrates one way of handling a difficult defense.

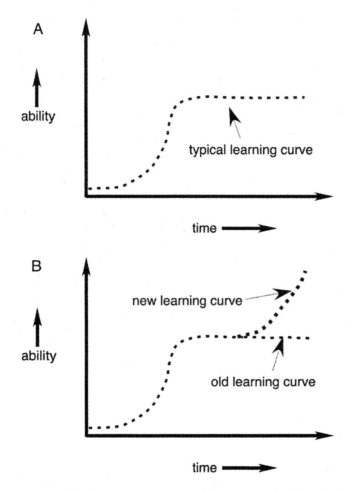

**Figure 25.1** - The learning curve. **A.** Graphical illustration of the initial rapid increase in learning a new task. This progress eventually saturates resulting in little progress after the initial rapid increase. The curve is an approximate sigmoidal function that is described generally by the equation: $A(t)=A(max) \times (1+e^{-B(S-St)})^{-1}$, where ability (A) is described as a function of time (t). **B.** By changing perspective, the saturation of the old learning curve can be overcome and a new learning curve established.

Clearly, several aspects of practicing can help you bring your game to the next level. But, in reality there is only so much you can practice by yourself at the table. If you are proficient at all the shots now, the best way for you to develop your game is simply to play a lot of games. Go out and play many different people, and you will encounter many different styles of play. At this point in your game, experience will help you infinitely more than just mere practice alone. New defenses you encounter will force you to bring your game to the next level. New offenses will cause you to hone your defense. Observing these different styles of play will allow you to incorporate elements into your game that you might not have thought of otherwise. In the end, the more you experience, the more robust will be your play.

# CHAPTER 26

# The Mental Side

Ahhhhhh, is this not where the essence of foosball dwells? Is not foosball a game in our minds? Through our easy 12-step program, you too will have prepared your mind for entrance into foosball heaven. You must first believe in yourself. If you don't believe that your shot will score, then why should it? You must be confident, but not cocky. Always remember to keep your focus on what you are doing. If you miss a shot, keep your cool. Don't worry. You'll get another chance. Just remember that scoring is a stochastic process. With that in mind (pun intended), here are a few suggested readings that go along with this chapter: the Bible, the Koran, and the Vedas. For if one can not understand the major religions of the world, how can one hope to understand the game of foosball?

Seriously though, as in any sport, a foosball competitor must not only be physically prepared for competition; he must also have the right mental attitude. In fact, the right mental attitude can often be more important than the most intense physical training. As the old adage says, "Whether you think you can or think you can't, you are absolutely right." This is indeed sound advice. We probably all have friends who have tremendous physical talent for the game, but who can never seem to break out of their routine and as a result are mediocre players. And, how many times have you personally missed a shot and then afterwards said, "I knew I was going to do that?" Chances are that you set yourself up for failure. You couldn't believe in your mind that you could make that shot, make that pass, or block that shot. So, your mind set your body up for the failure, and the chances of you executing the maneuver successfully were nil!

Sports psychologists have known this fact for years. In an experiment run at Caltech, psychologists tested a group of basketball players who were learning how to slam-dunk the ball, but were having problems executing properly. In one of the most telling trials in this experiment, they told one group of players that the rim had been lowered an imperceptible half-inch making it easier for them to dunk the ball. When the players attempted the dunk, almost all of them were able to complete dunks. In fact, it turns out that the height of the hoop had not been switched at all! To make this point even more clear, players that had been able to make dunks were told that the rim had been raised a half inch. All of a sudden, these players began to have troubles in their dunking. But, not only had the rim not been raised, it had in fact been lowered by a half-inch!

In analyzing high-resolution, computer-enhanced, slow-motion videos of these athletes, the researchers discovered several traits in those successfully dunking compared to those that did not. One of the most interesting observations was that the players who successfully dunked seemed relaxed. Well, that's as relaxed as you can be trying to make a dunk! But, the fact is that their body was executing maneuvers fluidly and without any extra expended energy. Their eyes were transfixed on the goal. And, they never stopped or hesitated. When asked what he was thinking about during the dunk, one athlete merely chuckled and said, "Making the shot and making it look good." He believed he was going to make the shot, and in the end he did. Even more importantly, he was having fun, and realized that it was all just a game.

Conversely, those who had difficulty dunking would show the opposite tendencies. They would look nervous, have several false starts, and their eyes would constantly wander around as if they were mentally unfocused. Their bodies appeared awkward and they "stretched" to make the dunk, as if they couldn't believe that it was in their normal capacity to make the shot…as if they needed some type of superhuman effort! When asked what they were thinking, most of these athletes responded by reciting a million different things that could go wrong while attempting the dunk. They took the shot too seriously and in the end the mental pressure to make the shot held them down more than gravity. When then told that the rim had been lowered even though it hadn't, their characteristics began to resemble those of the successful dunkers. When then asked what they were thinking, most said that it was a piece of cake to make the basket after it had been lowered.

So folks, it's clear that the mind is perhaps the biggest factor in determining our success in playing the game. All of the physical preparation in the world won't do you any good if you don't believe that you can make the shot. Maybe, you can empathize with some of these basketball players and see how negative thinking might affect your game. So, how do we bring about a positive mental attitude and bring our game up to the next level?

Well, several books have been written that are dedicated solely to this topic. And those seriously interested in the finer points of the mental game are encouraged to check them out. However, they all seem to agree on several main points.

First start by focusing, formulating strategies, reading the opponent; these skills are essential in playing the game. Visualization is key. Imagine the ball rocketing into the goal. Or, imagine making that outstanding defensive block. Once you can imagine yourself making those outstanding plays, the more likely you will be to actually make those outstanding plays.

Second, don't let the opponent distract you. Concentrate on what you want to do. Don't let the opponent taunt you into doing something. Play by your own will. As with the basketball players, don't concentrate on what can go wrong. Concentrate on what can go right!

Third, don't be afraid of failure. How many people let one missed shot, or block break them for the rest of the game? They agonize over that shot and play it over and over again even when there is nothing they can do about it. All the time, the game is still in progress and they can still come back and do something about it, but they give up because they're still stuck in the past. Learning how to not be afraid of failure and putting those events behind you is essential.

Fourth, be realistic. Understand your limitations and know what your body can do. If you haven't practiced a pull shot in over a year, don't expect to make one just because you believe you can. A healthy balance between a positive outlook and healthy realism makes for an outstanding fooshall player.

Fifth, keep your emotions in check. Sports in general bring out the competitive side in all of us, which is natural and healthy if kept in check. But, letting the game get out of hand and letting your emotions get the better of you hurts not only yourself but those you are playing with as well. Sometimes, we may "act" mad to show to the world that we could have made the shot. But as anyone who has traveled down this road will tell you, once you start acting upset then you start actually feeling upset. So, keep your perspective and emotions in check.

This leads to our final point. HAVE FUN! If you're not enjoying yourself, then what's the point of playing the game? When you're having fun and realize it's all a game, you will be more relaxed. Your mind will open up to the possibilities. You will be able to focus, and you won't be afraid of failure, because you'll know that it's all just a game. Furthermore, when we put these skills to use, that is when we derive true enjoyment from the sport.

# EPILOGUE

The foosball table is your world to lord over. You are the Creator of Shots and the Defender of Goals. Remember:

> Don't be afraid of missing a save,
> Don't be afraid of missing a shot,
> Bide your time, be brave;
> Stay cool, and soon you'll be hot.

# ABOUT THE AUTHOR

**Charles C. Lee** is an expert foosball player. He has played foosball competitively for over half a decade and competed in several tournaments. Players comment that his snake shot is one of the smoothest around the tables. When not playing foosball, he hosts a radio science program on KALX 90.7 FM in Berkeley, CA. Sometimes he also works on his Ph.D. in Neuroscience at the University of California at Berkeley.

**David Richard** is an expert foosball player. He has played competitively for several years and competed in several tournaments. He is well known for his lightning-fast pull shot. Currently, he spends time away from foosball working as an electrical engineer in Irvine, CA.

**Attma Sharma** is a master foosball player. He is well known for his excellent defense, and many games have been won by the solid nature of his play. Currently, he is an electrical engineer in Florida.

All three players met and refined their foosball skills in Lloyd House at the California Institute of Technology.

# APPENDIX I

## Official Rules of Foosball

### 1. To Start a Match

A coin flip shall precede the start of the match. The team that wins the flip has the choice of table side or first serve. The team that loses the flip has the remaining option and must also pay for the first game, with that expense alternating thereafter.

1. Once a team has chosen either the table side or the first serve, they may not change their decision.
2. In the event of the loser's bracket winner beating the winner's bracket team in the first match, the second match will be started in the same manner as a regular match with the coin flip, etc.
3. The match officially starts once the ball has been put into play. (BUT violations such as cursing, etc. may be called by the official assigned to judge the match as soon as he and both teams are present at the table.)

### 2. The Serve

A serve through the serving hole is used to put the ball into play at the start of the match, after a point is scored, or after a ball leaves the table. The server may attempt to influence the roll of the ball, but may not allow any part of either hand to be in the play area once the ball hits the playfield.

1.    The play area shall be defined as the area above the playing surface to the height of the side boards of the cabinet.

2.  Prior to serving the ball, the server may place either hand in the
    play area in order to position the ball.

3.  The ball may not be struck by either team following a serve until it
    has touched the playfield, at which time the ball is considered to
    be "in play" and the time limits start.

4.  Spinning the ball shall be allowed in order to influence the serve,
    however, no point shall be scored by the serving team unless the
    ball is struck by one of the serving team's figures.

5.  The server must not serve the ball until he has the assurance that
    the opposing team is ready for play to begin. The server can sig-
    nify that play is about to begin by tapping the ball on the side of
    the table.

    a. The server has tapped the ball, and the opposing team is
       holding their handles, the opposing team shall be deemed to
       be ready for play (unless they have specifically stated before
       the ball hits the playing surface that they are not ready yet).

6.  On the first violation of any part of this rule, the ball shall be re-
    served by the original server. Subsequent violations, however,
    shall result in the ball being put into play by a server of the oppos-
    ing team.

    a. If the ball is incorrectly served, but the server has not violated
       any part of these rules, the ball is considered in play. In par-
       ticular, the player may not reach into the play area to re-serve
       the ball (see 16).

## 3. Subsequent Serves

Following the first serve of a match, subsequent serves shall be made
by the team last scored upon. First serves in subsequent games of a

multi-game match shall be made by the team which lost the preceding game.

1. If the ball is served by the wrong team, and the violation is discovered before the ball is scored, play shall be stopped and the ball shall be re-served by the proper team. Once the ball is scored, no protests shall be allowed, and play shall continue as if no infraction had been committed.

2. If a team receives the serve because the opposing team is being penalized for a rules infraction, and if, after the ball is served, it goes dead or leaves the table and must be re-served, it shall be re-served by the team who originally served it prior to the infraction.

### 4. Ball in Play

Once a ball is put into play by the server (see 2), it shall remain in play until the ball is hit off the table, a dead ball is declared, time out is called, or a point is scored.

### 5. Ball Off the Table

If the ball should leave the playing area and strike the scoring marker, ash trays, top of the side rails, cabinet ends, or any object that is not a part of the table, the ball shall be declared off the table.

1. A ball which leaves the table as a result of a shot, pass, or any other form of clearing the ball from the two-rod, the ball will be played as follows: If the team which caused the ball to leave the table is the original server, then the ball will go back to that team's two-rod. If the team which caused the ball to leave the table is not the original server, then the other team shall serve the ball.

   a. In any other case of the ball leaving the table, it will be put back into play with a serve by the team which originally served the ball.

2. A ball entering the serving cup and then returning to the playfield is still considered "in play."

## 6. Dead Ball

A ball shall be declared a dead ball when it has completely stopped its motion and is not within reach of any player figure.

1. If the ball is declared dead anywhere between the two-man rods, it shall be put back into play with a serve by the team that originally served the ball.

2. If the ball is declared dead anywhere between the goal and the two-man rods, it shall be put back into play by placing the ball at the play figure nearest the spot of the dead ball.

   a. The goalie must have the assurance that the opposing team is ready for play to continue before putting the ball back into play in this manner (see 2.6). Furthermore, the goalie must then move the ball from one player figure to another one and then stop the ball for a full second before the motion of a shot or pass may begin.

3. The time limits begin one second after the ball touches the second man.

4. A ball that is spinning in place is not considered to be a dead ball.

5. A ball that is intentionally made dead in order to advance the ball or reset the time limits shall be given to the opposing team for a re-serve (example: the two-man placing the ball just out of reach in order to re-serve the ball).

6. The penalty for illegally putting the ball back into play (as in 6.2.a) is the opponent's choice of either continuing play from the current position or re-serving the ball. This includes the cases where a player either loses the ball or scores on himself before the ball has been put back into play.

## 7. Time Out

Each team is allowed two time outs per game during which the players may leave the table. Such time outs shall not exceed 30 seconds. If the ball is in play, time out may be called only by the team in possession of the ball, and then only if the ball is completely stopped. If the ball is not in play, either team may call time out.

1. Either team may take the full 30 seconds, even if the team that called the time out does not wish to take the full allotment.
2. Either team may switch positions during a time out (see 12).
3. A time out called between games shall apply to the following game to be played in counting time outs per game.
4. A player who removes both hands from the handles and turns completely away from the table while the ball is in play shall be considered to have requested a time out.
   a. A player can take his hands from the handles to wipe them off before a shot, as long as it doesn't take more than two or three seconds. However, all time limits continue to run while the player wipes his hands. The team on defense should not relax if the opponent takes his hand(s) off the rod (see 18.4).
5. Either team member may call time out when either he or his partner has the ball. The time out starts the moment the time out is called.
   a. If the team with the ball attempts a shot or pass immedieately after requesting a time out, the play shall not count, and the team shall be charged with a distraction (see 18) rather than a time out.
6. If the team in possession of the ball calls a time out while the ball is in play and moving, that team shall lose possession, and the ball shall be served by the opposing forward. If the team not in possession of the ball calls a time out when the ball is in play, that team shall be charged with a distraction (see 18.2).

7.  If a team is not ready to play at the end of the 30 second period, that team shall be charged with another time out.

8.  A team calling and/or charged with more than two time outs per game shall be charged with an automatic technical foul. The technical foul shall be shot before the 30 second period is granted.

    a.  A team charged with a time out shall always be given the full 30 second period, even if they have previously taken two time outs, and either team may switch positions during this time.

9.  Once a player begins to put the ball back into play following a time out (by moving the ball), a time out may not be called again until the ball has left the current rod of possession.

    a.  Penalty for violation of this rule (7.9) is loss of possession, and the ball shall be served by the opposing forward. The team shall not be charged with a time out.

10. During a time out a player may reach into the play area to spray the rods, wipe the playfield, etc. The ball may be picked up by hand, as long as it is returned to its original position before play is continued.

11. During a time out the player may not move the ball from man to man without the permission of the official, as this can be considered practice (see 19). Penalty for violation of this rule (7.11) is loss of possession and the ball shall be served by the opposing forward. If the official present feels that it would be impossible to be sure of accurately replacing the ball to the exact position it occupied at the time of a time out, they may deny a request to pick up the ball (example: a ball precariously perched on the edge of the goal).

## 8. Resuming Play After Time Out

Following a time out, the ball shall be put back into play by the player who had possession when the time out was called.

1. If the ball was in play when the time out was called, the player [B must have the assurance that the opposing team is ready before moving the ball. The player must then move the ball from one player figure to another one and then stop the ball for a full second before the motion of a shot or pass may begin.
   a. The time limit begins one second after the ball touches the second man.
2. If the ball was not in play when the time out was called, the ball shall be put back into play with a serve by the team that originally served that ball.
3. The penalty for illegally putting the ball back into play is the opponent's choice of either continuing play from the current position or re-serving the ball. This includes the case of a player losing the ball before touching two men.

### 9. Official Time Out

An official time out does not count towards the two time outs allowed per team per game. After an official time out, the ball is put back into play as though a regular time out were called.
1. If an official is not present at the start of the match, and a dispute arises during play, either team may request an official. Such a request can be made at any point during the match that the ball is stopped or dead.
   a. The first request for an official is considered an official time out. The cost for the official will be split between the two teams.
   b. If the defensive team makes a request for an official while the ball is in play and stopped, and the offensive team simultaneously attempts a pass or shot, the request for a time out will be treated as a distraction by the defensive team. Likewise, a

request for an official while the ball is in motion will also be considered a distraction.

1. Any team subsequently requesting an official will automatically be charged with a time out. Such a request may only be made during a dead ball. The penalty for requesting another official while the ball is in play is a technical foul.

   a. The Head Official will decide whether the request for a new official will be granted. If the request is granted, the team requesting the official must pay the full cost of the new official. The two officials will then judge the match. An official may be replaced only at the discretion of the Head Official.

   b. If there are already two officials present, any request for a new official will be denied, and the team will be charged with a technical foul.

3. A team may not switch positions during an official time out, unless they are otherwise entitled to do so (see 12).

4. Table Maintenance—Any necessary table maintenance, such as changing balls, tightening the men, etc., must be requested before the start of the match. The only time that a player may call a table maintenance time out during a match would be in the case of a sudden alteration to the table, such as a broken man, broken screw, crumbling bumper, bent rod, etc.

   a. If a player figure is broken while in contact with the ball, an official time out will be declared while the rod is fixed. Play will resume on the rod where the player figure broke.

   b. If the table lighting fails, play shall immediately stop at that point (as though an official time out were called).

   c. Routine maintenance, such as spraying the rods, etc., should only be done during time outs and between games.

5. Foreign objects on field of play—if an object should fall on the playfield, play shall immediately stop at that point. There should

be nothing on the ends of the table that could fall onto the playfield.

6. Medical time out—a player or team may request a medical time out. This request must be approved by the Tournament Director, the Head Official, and a member of the officiating staff. They will determine the length of the medical time out, up to a maximum or 60 minutes. A player who is physically unable to continue playing after that time must forfeit the match.

   a. If the request for a medical time out is denied, the player will be charged with a time out. The player may also be penalized for delay of game (see 24), at the discretion of the official.

   b. Medical time outs will typically be granted only for accidental or unexpected injuries incurred during the course of play.

## 10. Point Scored

A ball entering the goal shall count as a point, as long as it was legally scored. A ball which enters the goal but returns to the playing surface and/or leaves the table still counts as a goal.

1. If a point is not counted on the scoring markers and both teams agree that it was previously scored and inadvertently not marked up, the point shall count. If both teams do not agree that a point was scored and not marked up, after another ball is scored, that point shall not be counted.

2. If there is a controversy over whether or not the ball entered the goal, an official should be called.

3. Any team intentionally marking up a point not scored shall not get credit for the point illegally marked up and shall be charged with a technical foul. Further violations of this rule will be grounds for forfeiture of game or match (to be determined by the Head Official).

## 11. Table Sides

At the end of each game, teams must switch sides of the table before play of the next game can begin. A maximum of 60 seconds is allowed between games.

1. Either team can request the full 60 seconds. If both teams acknowledge that they are ready to resume play before the full time is used, play shall continue and the remainder of that 60 seconds is then forfeited.
2. If a team, is not ready to play at the end of the 60 second period, that team shall be charged with delay of game.

## 12. Change of Positions

In any doubles event, each player may play only the two rods normally designated for his position. Once the ball is put into play, the players must play the same position until a point is scored, a team requests a time out, or a technical is called.

1. Either team may switch positions during a time out, between points, between games, or before and/or after a technical foul shot.
2. Once a team has switched positions, they may not switch back until after the ball has been put back into play or another time out has been called.
   a. A team is considered to have switched positions once both players are in their respective places facing the table.
3. Illegally switching positions while the ball is in play will be judged a distraction.
   a. In any doubles event any player placing their hand on any rod normally designated as one played by their partner while the ball is in play shall be judged as a distraction violations.

## 13. Spinning the Rods

Spinning of the rods is illegal. Spinning is defined as the rotation of any soccer figure more than 360 degrees before or after striking the ball. In calculating the 360 degrees, you do not add the degrees spun prior to striking the ball to the degrees spun after striking the ball.

1. A ball which is advanced by an illegal spin is replayed as follows: If the ball goes in the goal, then it will not be counted as a point and will be put back into play by the goalie as if the ball had been declared a dead ball between the goal and the nearest two-man rod. If the ball does not go in the goal, the opposing team will have the option of continuing play from the current position or re-serving the ball.

2. Spinning of a rod which does not advance and/or strike the ball does not constitute an illegal spin. If a player's spinning rod hits the ball backwards into his own goal, it will count as a goal for the opposing team. Spinning of a rod away from the ball (when there is no possession) is not considered an illegal spin, but may be ruled as a distraction.

3. If an ungrasped rod is spun by the force of a ball hitting a player figure on the rod, the spin will be considered legal (example: a two-man shot in singles hitting the three-man).

## 14. Jarring

Any jarring, sliding, or lifting of the table shall be illegal. Whether or not the table jarring is done intentionally is of no consequence. This call must be made by an official. It is not necessary for a player to lose the ball for jarring to be called on his opponent.

1. The penalty for violation of this rule: First offense—the opposing team has the option of continuing play from the current position, continuing play from the point of infraction, or re-serving the ball. If an illegal jar causes the player to lose possession of the ball

from a rod, play may be continued from that rod. Subsequent violations—Technical foul. After the technical shot the non offending team continues to have the options listed under First Offense (14.1).

2. Touching or coming into contact with your opponent's rods in any way shall be penalized exactly like jarring, sliding, or lifting.

3. Jarring of the table may be called even if the ball is not in play. In particular, slamming the rod after the shot may be considered jarring.

## 15. Reset

If a player has the ball stopped and set up to shoot or pass, and the ball is unintentionally moved due to jarring by the opponent, the official present will call "reset" and he will reset all time limits. The player with the ball has the option of setting the ball up again, or ignoring the reset call and playing the ball where it is.

1. Any movement of the ball, no matter how slight, may be considered grounds for a reset (example: a ball rocking in place).

2. A reset is not considered a distraction, and the player with the ball may shoot immediately. The defensive team should not, therefore, relax or look at the official upon hearing the word "reset," but rather should stay on defense.

3. A reset call does not count as jarring infraction, however, repeated offenses may be grounds for the official present to call a technical foul on the defensive player causing the reset.

4. A reset violation behind the ball shall not be considered a reset violation. It shall be considered a jarring violation. (Example: if the opposing forward is judged to have reset his opponent when the opponent has the ball on the 3 rod.)

5. An intentional reset by the team in possession of the ball for the purposes of attempting to get a reset call from the official shall

not be allowed. The team judged to be in violation of this rule shall lose possession of the ball, the ball to be reserved by the other team. (This is not counted as a reset.)

6. A team is allowed one reset call per game. After that, a team causing two resets during the same point will be charged with a technical foul.
   a. If a technical foul is called for excessive resets, the next reset call shall not result in a technical foul.
   b. Resets are charged per-team and not per-player.
7. If the defender intentionally jars the table, this will not be considered a reset, and jarring will be called immediately.
8. If the defender intentionally jars the table, this will not be considered a reset, and jarring will be called immediately.

## 16. Reaching Into the Playing Area

It is illegal for a player to reach into the play area while the ball is in play without first having permission from the opposing team, whether he touches the ball or not. However, whenever the opposing team grants a player permission to reach into the playing area, it is legal for the player to do so.

1. A spinning ball is considered "in-play," even if it is not in reach of a player figure. It is illegal to reach into playing area to stop a spinning ball, even if done for an opponent.
2. A ball which becomes airborne over the table is still in play until it has hit something not a part of the playing area. Do not catch a flying ball over the table.
3. A ball which has gone dead is considered out of play. The ball may be freely touched once permission has been granted by the official, or if no official is present, by the opposing team.

4. A player may wipe shot marks off any part of the table while the ball is not in play. He does not need to ask permission of the opposing team.

5. The penalty for violation of this rule is as follows: If the player has possession of the ball, and the ball is stopped—loss of possession to the opposing team. If the ball is moving in the player's goal area behind the two-man rod—a point is scored for the opposing team, and the ball is re-served as if it had gone in the goal. Any other case—technical foul.

## 17. Alterations to the Table

Playing area—no changes can be made that would affect the interior playing characteristics of the table by any player. This includes changes to the men, playing surface, bumpers, etc.

1. A player cannot wipe sweat or spit or any foreign substance on his hand before wiping ball marks off the table.
    a. Wiping rosin on the table is illegal.
    b. Any player using a substance on their hands to improve their grip, for example, must make sure that this substance does not get on the ball. If this does occur, and the substance is judged to affect the play of the ball (Example: a ball coated with rosin) that ball and any others in the table similarly affected shall be cleaned immediately and the team judged to have caussed this to occur shall be penalied for delay of game and warned that if this occurs again during the match they will be prohibited from using the substance.

2. Handles—in regard to the use of substances to improve grip, if a player uses a substance that, upon switching tables sides, has left a deposit on the handles, he must immediately clean the handles.

a. If the time necessary to remove the substance exceeds 60 seconds, the player will be penalized for delay of game, and the player will be prohibited from using the substance again.

3. A player may not place a tube or handle on the table exterior that inhibits the motion of the rods (example: for limiting the motion of the goalie rod).

4. A player may not switch the handles on the exterior of the tables.

5. A request to change balls before the start of the match must be approved by the official present or the Tournament Director. The request will be granted only if the playing characteristics of the existing balls are significantly different from the standard.

   a. New ball—a player may not ask for a new ball while the ball is in play. During a dead ball, however, a player may request a new ball from the rack inside the table. Such a request will generally be granted, unless the official present judges that such a request is made simply for the purpose of stalling play.

   b. A player requesting a new ball while the ball is in play shall be charged with a time out, unless the official present judges the ball to be unplayable, in which case no time out will be charged.

6. Unless otherwise specified, penalty for violation of any part of this rule may be grounds for a technical foul.

## 18. Distraction

Any movement or sound made away from the rod where the ball is in play may be judged as a distraction. No point made as a result of a distraction will count. If a player believes he is being distracted, it is his responsibility to call for an official.

1. Banging the five-man rod or any rod prior to, during, or after a shot is considered a distraction. Moving the five man slightly after the shot has started is not considered a distraction, however.

2. Talking between teammates while the ball is in play may be judged a distraction.

3. It is not considered a distraction, when passing, to move the catching rod as part of a fake. Excessive motion, however, is grounds for a distraction.

4. It is considered a distraction, after setting up a shot, to remove a hand from the handle and then shoot the ball. The ball may only be shot after the hand/wrist has been on the handle for a full second.

   a. In singles, rule 18.4 only applies to a set shot on the three-rod.

5. Penalty for distraction—if a shot is scored as a result of a distraction by the offensive team, the point will not count and the opposing team will re-serve the ball. In all other cases, the opposing team has the option of continuing play from the current position, continuing play from the point of infraction, or re-serving the ball. Subsequent violations may be grounds for a technical foul.

## 19. Practice

Once a match has begun, no player may practice either his serve or shot on either the table being played or on any other table. This rule applies during time outs and between games.

1. Practice is defined as either moving the ball (by contacting it with a player figure) or practicing the serve.

   a. Illegal Practice is a judgement call by th official present at the table. Inadvertent movement of th ball does not necessarily constitute Practice.

2. Penalty for this infraction is a technical foul, except in the case of putting the ball back into play following a time out (see 7.11).

## 20. Language

Unsportsmanlike comments made directly or indirectly by a player are not allowed. Violations of this rule may be grounds for a technical foul.

1. Calling the attention of the opposing team away from the game is not allowed (see 18). Any shouts or sounds made during a match, even if of an enthusiastic nature, may be grounds for a technical foul.
2. Cursing by a player shall not be allowed. Continued cursing by a player may be cause for forfeiture of games and/or expulsion from the tournament site.
3. The use of a spotter in the audience shall not be allowed. Furthermore, a member of the audience is not allowed to influence a match by distracting a player or official. Violation of this rule may be grounds for expulsion of the person from the tournament site.
4. Coaching will be allowed, but only during time outs and inbetween games.

## 21. Passing

1. A pinned ball on the 5 man cannot be directly advanced to the 3 man rod of the same team. It must touch at least two player figures as it is put into the motion of a pass (Except an accidental stub or squib pass SEE 21.1c). A pinned ball is on that is pinned to the wall or playfield.
   a. A ball whose motion has clearly stopped may be legally passed if this pass if immediate. Any hesitation befor the pass and the pass shall be declared illegal. Once a ball has clearly stopped and is not immediately passed it must then touch at least two player figures before it can be legally passed.

b. Changing the lateral speed or direction of the ball from the front or back of the man prior to passing the ball is considered to be an adjustment and is illegal. Changing the speed or direction of the ball from the side of the man is legal.

c. An accidental stub or squib pass is legal. However, if a ball is stubbed or squibbed by a player figure, released, and then passed by that player figure before striking another player figure on that same rod, it is illegal.

2. A pinned or stopped ball may be shot on goal, to be considered a shot, the ball must either go into the goal, be blocked by the opposing goalie's men, or hit the back wall. If the atte[Bmpted shot is blocked by the opposing five-man rod and then caught by the shooter's three-man, It shall be declared an illegal pass.

a. If a pinned or stopped ball from the five-man is shot on goal, and the ball hits the shooter's three-man row, then the shot would be legal, provided the ball was not caught by the three-man.

b. A caught ball is defined as a ball that is in the possession of a rod long enough for a controlled pass or shot to be attempted (examples: pick-up and quick shots).

3. Before attempting a pass from the five-man rod, the player cannot make the ball strike the side wall of the table more than twice. It makes no difference which wall the ball touches—a total of two times is all that is allowed. If the ball goes to the wall a third time, it must be advanced in the motion of a pass or shot.

a. Defensive trap—if an opponent's pass or shot is stopped by trapping it against the side wall, that does not count as one of the two times allowed to touch the wall by the player who made the trap and is now in possession of the ball on his five-man rod.

    **b.** Once the ball has touched the wall, it will not be counted as hitting the wall again until the ball has rolled off the side strip (if present on the table).

    **c.** Following a time-out, any strike the ball makes against the wall prior to touching a second man will not be counted against the allowed two strikes.

4. Passing from the two-man and goalie rods—rule 21.1 also applies to a pass from the two-man or goalie rod to the same team's five-man rod. However, once a ball is forwarded from either the two-man or the goalie rods, if it should strike an opposing team's player figures, that ball is no longer considered a pass but a live ball that may be legally caught by any player.

    **a.** Rule 21.2a also applies here for a stopped shot from the two-man touched by the five-man.

5. It is legal to have just one hand on the rods when playing defensive (example: right hand on defensive five man) It is also legal to use two hands to move a rod (example: defensive five-man).

6. Penalty for an illegal pass— if a team violates the above rule of passing, the opposing team has the option of continuing play from the current position or re-serving the ball.

## 22. Time of Possession

Possession of the ball at any one rod shall be limited to 15 seconds, except the five-man rod which has a ten second limit, by the end of which time period the player in possession must advance the ball to or past at least one rod of the opposing team.

1. Advancement defined: A ball is considered to have advanced once it is out of reach of the player figures on that rod whether it went forward or backwards. In the case of the goalie area, a ball is considered advanced once out of reach of the player figures on the two-rod and beyond the goal area.

2. Enforcement of the time of possession rule shall be made only by a certified tournament offical.

3. A spinning ball that is within reach of a player figure shall be considered to be in that rod's possession and all time limits shall continue. Players must make an honest effort to gain possession of a spinning ball that is within reach, however, if the spinning ball is not within reach, the time limits are not in effect.

4. Penalty—penalty for three-man delay is loss of possession to the opposing goalie. The goalie shall put the ball back into play as if it had been declared a dead ball. Penalty for delay at any other rod is loss of possession to the opposing forward for serve.

## 23. Match Time Limit

Best of five matches shall be limited to one hour of play from the time the match is started. Best of three matches shall be limited to 35 minutes from the time the match is started.

1. If the specified time limit expires before the match has been completed, an official will announce to the players that a ten minute overtime period will begin at that time. If the overtime period ends before the match has been completed, the winner of the match shall be the player or team which has won the most games, or if the teams have an equal number of games, it shall be the team that has scored the most points in the game in progress, after the ball in play at this time that the overtime period expires has been scored. If the teams have won an equal number of games and scored an equal number of points after this ball has been scored, one more ball shall be played to determine the winner of the match.

2. Time outs called within the regular time limit of a match shall be counted against the total amount of time left to play. However,

time outs do not count against the ten minutes in the overtime period (a time out would then stop the clock).

3. Official time outs do not count against the total amount of time left to play.

4. Enforcement of this rule is the responsibility or the Tour nt Director.

## 24. Delay of Game

Play shall be continuous, except during time outs. A delay of game penalty may only be called by an official.

1. After a delay of game infraction play shall resume in at most 10 seconds. At the end of 10 seconds another delay of game call should be made.

2. Taking too much time to serve the ball or to put the ball back into play may be grounds for delay of game.

3. The first infraction of this rule is a warning. Subsequent infractions will result in the player being charged with a time out. Example: Player charged with delay of game. If still not ready to resume play after 10 seconds— time out charged. If after the time out still not ready, another 10 seconds—second time out charged (See 7.8).

## 25. Forfeiture

Once a match has been called, both teams should report immediately to the designated table. If a team has not reported to the table within three minutes, they should be recalled. A team, upon being recalled, must report immediately to the table in order to stop the forfeiture process.

1. A recall is made every three minutes. Penalty for second and subsequent recalls is forfeiture of a game.

2. If a team has forfeited any games due to recalls, they get the choice of side or serve once play begins.
3. Enforcement of this rule is the responsibility of the Tournament Director.

## 26. Technical Fouls

If, in the judgment of an authorized tournament official, either team competing in a match is at any time in flagrant or intentional violation of these rules of play, a technical foul may be called on the offending team.

1. When a technical foul is called, play shall stop and the ball awarded to the opponents of the offending team at its three-man rod. One shot will be taken after which play shall stop. If it scores or not, the ball shall be put back into play at the spot it was when the technical was called. If the ball was in motion, it will be put back into play as if it had been declared dead at that spot. (Except as provided in 14.1).
    a. A player is considered to have taken a technical foul shot once ball has left the three-man rod. A player is considered to have been blocked the shot once the ball has either stopped in or left the defender's area.
2. On a technical foul shot, the ball must be put into play before shooting (see 8.1). Furthermore, all rules, including time limits and resets, still apply.
3. A team may switch positions before and/or after the technical foul shot without being charged with a time out (see 12).
4. Time outs may be called during a technical shot, as long as they would otherwise be legal (see 7).
5. A point scored on an illegal technical shot shall not be allowed, and play shall resume at the spot the technical was called.

6. If a technical foul shot ends the game, the opposing team gets the first serve of the next game.
7. Further violations of a flagrant or intentional nature shall carry additional technical fouls. A third technical foul in any one game shall result in an automatic forfeiture of the game. Also, the official may announce at any time after the first technical foul is called on a team that further violation by that team shall be cause for forfeiture of the game or match.

## 27. Rules Decisions and Appeals

If a controversy involves a question of judgement, and the official is present at the time the events in question transpired, his decision is final and no appeal may be made. If the controversy involved an interpretation of the rules, or the official was not present at the time the events in question transpired, the official shall make the most equitable decision possible under the circumstances. Decisions of this nature may be appealed, but it must be done immediately in the manner prescribed below.

1. In order to appeal a rule interpretation, a player must file that appeal with the official before the ball being played at the time of the controversy is put back into play. An appeal concerning the loss of a match must be filed before the team that won has begun its next match.
2. All rule appeals shall be considered by the Head Official and (if present) at least two members of the officiating staff. All decisions on appeals are final.
3. A team making an unsuccessful rules appeal of an obvious nature, or a team that questions a judgment call, will be charged with a time out. In addition, the team may also be penalized for delay of game, at the discretion of the official.

4. Arguing with a Certified official during a match will not be allowed. Violation of this rule will be grounds for a delay of game penalty and/or a violation of the code of ethics.

## 28. Code of Ethics

Any action of an unsportsmanlike or unethical nature during tournament play, in the tournament room, or on the grounds of the host facility, will be considered a violation of the Code of Ethics.

1. Penalty—the penalty for breaking the Code or Ethics may be forfeiture of a game or match, expulsion from the tournament, and/or a fine. Whether or not the Code of Ethics has been broken, and what is the appropriate penalty for the infraction will be determined by the Disciplinary Committee of the USTSA.

## 29. Tournament Director

The administration of tournament play shall be the responsibility of the Tournament Director. This includes making the draws, scheduling the events, timing matches, etc. The decision of the Tournament Director in such matters is final.

1. All matters pertaining to rules of play (appointing officials, handling appeals, etc.) shall be the responsibility of the Head Official. The Tournament Director is responsible for appointing the Head Official.

## Goalie Wars

Goalie Wars is a singles specialty event where the three and five-man rods are lifted up, and the defenders play against each other.

1. **The Serve**

   The ball must touch two men and then be stopped for a full second before a shot may be attempted. Violation is loss of possession.

   1. Time limits start one second after the ball has touched the second man.

2. **Possession**

   In order to shoot the ball and score a point, a player must have possession of the ball. If the ball is in a player's defensive area, that player has possession of the ball. However, if the ball is in the center of the table, the player who last had the ball in his defensive area loses possession of the ball to the other player.

   1. A player's defensive area is defined to extend from the back wall to the end of where the two-man rod reaches. The center of the table is the remaining area of play.

   2. A ball that strikes any rod, player figure, or bumper in the center of the table is still considered a live ball. These rods play no part in determining possession of the ball.

   3. If a ball leaves the playing area and strikes a foreign object, the ball is re-served by the player who originally served the ball. If a ball goes dead on the table, the ball is re-served by the player who has possession of the ball.

   4. If player A shoots a ball that never reaches player B's defensive area, player A must first stop or control the ball, and then give the ball back to player B to re-serve. In particular, a shot that bounces back and goes in the shooter's goal counts, since that player must first stop and control the ball.

3. **Time Limits**

   There is a ten second possession limit in the defensive area. In addition, once the ball is stopped or pinned for more than three seconds, three ball must be moved to another man before a shot is attempted.

4. **Time Outs**

You are allowed two time outs per game.


### Four-on-Four

Four on Four is a specialty event where there are four players on a side, with each player holding a single rod.

**1. Change of Positions**

1. If a team scores a point, they must rotate positions before the next point: the player on the three-man rod moves to the goalie-rod, while the players on the goalie, two-man, and five-man rods move to the two-man, five-man, and three-man rods respectively.

2. A team may also change positions before the start of the match or between games. However, no other changes of positions will be allowed.

**2. Legal Shots**

1. The game is played rollerball style, i.e., a ball may not be pinned for more than three seconds or stopped for more than one second, and there is a ten second time limit per rod.

2. Once a ball is stopped or pinned, the player must make sure the ball touches another man of the same team (on any rod) in order to score a point.

3. If a point is scored illegally, the ball shall be re-served by the opposing team.

**3. Time Outs**

You are allowed two time outs.

# Appendix II

# Additional Resources

*The Compete Book of Foosball* by Johnny Lott with Kathy Brainard.

This is the only other book ever written on foosball and is an excellent resource if you can find it. However, it is currently out of print. And, much of the material relates to the old Tournament Soccer Tables.

The North American Table Soccer Association
http://www.natsa.org

This organization sponsors tournaments and is responsible for organizing competitions throughout North America. It is also responsible for promoting the game of foosball. Their web site is full of useful information.

# GLOSSARY

**Aardvark**—A big furry mammal that burrows and eats ants. I've never seen one, but I'm fairly confident that they can't play foosball. Still, much zen wisdom might be obtained from such noble, burrowing creatures.

**Angle Shot**—Any shot where the ball is lauched at an angle. More specifically, refers to a technique used in conjunction with the pass kick (Ch. 16)

**Back-pin**—A pin position where the ball is trapped against the front side of the playing figure and the table. See also front-pin. (Ch. 7)

**Back-pin-pull**—A shot that starts from the back-pin position and finishes in the pull hole. (Ch. 17)

**Back-pin-push**—A shot that starts from the back-pin position and finishes in the push hole. (Ch. 17)

**Ball**—Round, spherical object used to play foosball. The object of the game is to place the ball in the goal. I really shouldn't have to explain this, unless you are suffering from a massive head wound. (Ch. 3)

**Ball Control**—The ability to manipulate the ball's movement at will. This too should have been readily obvious to anyone whose diet doesn't include Kentucky Fried Aardvark. (Ch. 8)

**Bank Shot**—An angled shot that first rebounds off of a side wall before entering the goal. (Ch. 21)

**Brush Pass**—A pass that makes use of the brush stroke. (Ch. 11)

**Brush Stroke**—A technique used to impart side spin to the ball. (Ch. 11)

**Closed Stance**—A stance where the body facing away from the goal. See also Open Stance. (Ch. 4)

**Coin Flip**—The means used to decide who serves first and which side of the table is taken. It involves the use of a coin. It also involves someone flipping the coin. If a coin is unavailable or no one posesses coin-flipping skills, a suitable random, binary number generator may be used. (Ch. 3)

**Defense**—The position involving the use of the Two-Man and Goalie Rods. The role of the defense is to prevent the offense from placing the ball in goal. See also Offense. (Ch. 3)

**Double Pass Kick**—A pass kick that involves passing the ball twice before striking the ball. (Ch. 17)

**Doubles Match**—A game of foosball where two teams comprised of two players compete against one another. See also Singles Match. (Ch. 3)

**Dribbling**—Any maneuver that involves passing the ball repetitively back-and-forth between two playing figures. (Ch. 12)

**Fair Serve**—A serve which does not give an advantage to either side. (Ch. 6)

**Figure**—Plastic objects attached to the rods which are used to manipulate the movement of the ball. To me, these playing figures bear some small resemblance to Sigmund Freud, but that might just be my id talking. (Ch. 3)

**Five-Man Rod**—The rod located nearest the center of the table. It is one of two rods used in the offense. See also Three-Man Rod. (Ch.3)

**Five-Man Turnaround**—A turnaround pass where the ball is passed to the center five-man before being passed forward. See also Lane-Angled Pass and Wall-Bounce Pass. (Ch. 11)

**Foosball**—German word for soccer. Sprechen Sie Deutsch? Also, the common name for Table Soccer. (Ch. 1)

**Forward Rod**—See Three-Man Rod. (Ch. 3)

**Front-pin**—A pin position where the ball is trapped against the back side of the figure and the table. See also Back-pin. (Ch.

**Front-pin Series**—A series of shots that start from the front-pin position. (Ch. 18)

**Front-pin-pull**—A shot that starts from the front-pin position and finishes in the pull hole. (Ch.18)

**Front-pin-push**—A shot that starts from the front-pin position and finishes in the push hole. (Ch.18)

**Goal**—One of two openings located at each end of the foosball table. The object of the game is to place the ball in this opening. Of course, you certainly have the option of not placing the ball in the goal. After all, isn't zen about the process of doing and not of achieving? (Ch. 3)

**Goalie Rod**—The rod closest to the goal which is comprised of three playing figures. It is one of the two rods used in defense. See also Two-Man Rod. (Ch. 3)

**Golf Grip**—A grip technique which provides moderate stability and moderate flexibility for manipulating the rods. See also Power Grip and Palm Grip. (Ch. 5)

**Grok**—To understand completely. Also found in the name of my radio show, "Berkeley Groks", which airs on KALX 90.7 FM in Berkeley, CA. See also Perspicacity.

**Handle**—Wooden object attached to the rods on the outside of the table enabling manipulation of the rods. Again, this should be obvious, unless you've been mauled by a pack of ill-tempered hyenas. (Ch. 3)

**Lane**—The space between two defending figures on the same rod. See also Wall. (Ch.10)

**Lane Pass**—Any pass that travels between two defending figures. See also Wall Pass. (Ch. 10)

**Lane-Angled Pass**—A turnaround pass where the ball is angled through the lane. See also Wall-Bounce Pass and Five-Man Turnaround. (Ch. 11)

**Lane-Brush Pass**—A pass through the lane which makes use of the brush stroke. See also Wall-Brush Pass. (Ch. 11)

**Life**—Ah, indeed! What is the meaning of Life? Across rampant, unkempt isolation, we wait for absolution. Trembling at the glare of unknown certainty. Railing against the recalcitrance of superfluous pleas. Oh, Absalom! Wrought with such earnest queries! Speak now of eviscerated pride! Direct your attention heavenward and see that god that we have created struggling for a glimpse of infinity. That sallow, jaundiced yearning caught in a moment stretched outward as it toys with the dying embers of a thousand, sullen supernovas, creating forever a moment frozen for eternity's earnest ending, and revealing the recollected awakening to a dappled morning dew. Recall, one morn, those barren, sullen fields of Utah's sinuous countenance as it stealthily crept inward into the glory of an ill-prepared sun. Cautiously, the wistful warmth tightened its grasp, and in that moment, time expanded outward with the unparalleled force of countless lives branching from the nodes of an aeolian ether. The fury of nature's fusillade evinced that the time of reckoning within the soul had become a landscape replete with the culmination of so many lives bought and paid. Oh, those hues of amber and rosemary which coveted this barren vista! Barren no longer by electric realization winding its grasp into the fiber of being. Life held precariously eternal in a moment so suddenly slipping away. That moment when all was right becoming ever less recognizable. So suddenly gone as though never in my grasp. Just a faint glimmer. A memory. As if it never existed. Much as I don't now.

Line-up—A specific configuration of playing figures. (Ch.20)

Middle Hole—The middle of the goal. See also Pull Hole and Push Hole. (Ch. 13)

NATSA—Acronym for the North American Table Soccer Association, an organization that sponsors tournaments and promotes the game of foosball. (Ch. 1)

Offense—The position involving the use of the Five-Man and Three-Man Rod. The role of the offense is to place the ball in the goal. See also Defense. (Ch. 3)

Open Stance—A stance where the body faces towards the goal. See also Closed Stance. (Ch. 4)

**Option**—Any of the possible choices available for a shot or pass. (Ch. 17)

**Option Shot**—Any shot capable of hitting multiple holes in the goal from the same starting position. See also Speed Shot. (Ch. 13)

**Own-goal**—Any maneuver that places the ball in your own goal. Isn't funny how most of these definitions are self-explnatory? Do you think it reflects some fundamental order to the universe? (Ch. 19)

**Palm Grip**—A grip technique which provides low stability and high flexibility for manipulating the rods. See also Golf Grip and Power Grip. (Ch. 5)

**Pass Kick**—A technique where the ball is first passed between figures before being shot at the goal. (Ch. 16)

**Peppard, Lee**—Designer of the Tournament Soccer line of foosball tables. I've never met him, but I heard that he is a nice guy, though not as noble as an aardvark. (Ch. 2)

**Perspicacity**—Acute perceptiveness. Also, the name of the first novel I ever wrote. One day, I'll try to publish it after some massive editing. See also Grok.

**Pin**—A position where the ball is trapped between the playing figure and the table. (Ch. 7)

**Power Grip**—A grip technique which provides high stability and low flexibility for manipulating the rods. See also Golf Grip and Palm Grip. (Ch. 5)

**Pull Hole**—The side of the goal closest to the offense player. See also Middle Hole and Push Hole. (Ch. 13)

**Pull Shot**—Any shot that enters the Pull Hole. More specifically, also refers to a specific shot that involves pulling the rod. See also Push Shot. (Ch. 15)

**Push Hole**—The side of the goal closest to the defense player. See also Middle Hole and Push Hole. (Ch. 13)

**Push Shot**—Any shot that enters the Push Hole. More specifically, also refers to a specific shot that involves pushing the rod. See also Pull Shot. (Ch. 15)

**Race Defense**—A defense strategy where the defender attempts to race the offense player to the goal. See also Stochastic Defense (Ch.20)

**Rattle**—A technique used with the snake shot where the ball is rocked from side-to-side in order to disguise the intended direction of the shot. (Ch. 14)

**Reverse Shot**— Any shot involving a switch in direction of the shot. See also Turnaround Pass. (Ch. 17)

**Rod**—Any of the thin metal tubes on which the playing figures are attached. Also useful for roasting an aardvark over a campfire. (Ch. 3)

**Service Cup**—A bowl-like protrusion surrounding the service hole found on some foosball tables. (Ch. 6)

**Singles Match**—A one-on-one game of foosball. See also Doubles Match. (Ch. 3)

**Slide Series**—A series of passes that include the straight wall and lane passes. (Ch. 10)

**Snake Shot**—A special offensive shot that involves full rotation of the playing figure. It combines speed with multiple options. (Ch. 14)

**Speed Shot**—A shot that relies on speed to beat the defense. Aptly named, don't you think? (Ch. 13)

**Spray**—Any shot or pass whose trajectory is not completely controlled. Also refers to shots and passes that miss their target. (Ch. 17)

**Stochastic Defense**—A defense strategy that involves randomized movement of the men. See also Race Defense. (Ch. 22)

**Table Soccer**—see Foosball. (Ch. 1)

**Tango Pass Series**—A series of passes used to move the ball from the defense to the offense. (Ch. 12)

**Three-Man Rod**—The rod located closest to the opponent's two-man rod. This rod contains three playing figures and is one of two rods used in the offense. Also known as the Forward Rod. See also Five-Man Rod. (Ch.3)

**Tornado Soccer Company**—Manufacturers of the Tornado Soccer Tables used by the USTSA. (Ch. 1)

**Tournament Soccer Company**—Company founded by Lee Peppard which produced the Tournament Soccer Tables used by the WTSA. (Ch. 1)

**Turnaround Pass**—Any pass involving a switch in direction of the pass. See also Reverse Shot. (Ch. 11)

**Two-Man Rod**—The defensive rod located next to the goalie rod which is comprised of two playing figures. It is one of the two rods used in defense. See also Goalie Rod. (Ch. 3)

**Uppity**—Arrogant. A characteristic unbecoming a foosball player, or anyone for that matter. It is also the word that kept me from advancing in the Arizona Spelling Bee. Ironic, don't you think? Excuse me while I have a moment of cathartic release. Arghhh! Now, the healing can begin.

**USTSA**—Acronym for United States Table Soccer Association, the professional group that used the Tornado Soccer Tables. (Ch. 1)

**Verisimilitude**—Something which on the surface appears to be true. This has nothing to do with foosball. I just like the word. It has a nice ring to it.

**Wall**—The side of the foosball table. Also used to define the area between the side of the table and the first playing figure on the rod. See also Lane. (Ch. 10)

**Wall Pass**—Any pass that travels along the side wall of the table. See also Lane Pass. (Ch. 10)

**Wall-Bounce Pass**—A turnaround pass where the ball bounces off the wall. See also Lane-Angled Pass and Five-Man Turnaround. (Ch.10)

**Wall-Brush Pass**—A pass along the wall that makes use of the brush stroke. See also Lane-Brush Pass. (Ch. 11)

**Wrist Flick**—A technique involving a quick snap of the wrist which forcefully impacts the playing figure against the ball. (Ch. 5)

**WTSA**—Acronym for World Table Soccer Association, the professional group that used the Tournament Soccer Tables. (Ch. 1)

**Zen**—A form of Buddhism that uses introspection as a means to attaining enlightenment, characterized best by the noble, ant-eating, burrowing creature, the aardvark.

0-595-21705-2